The Spirit of Faith

If You Knew What Was on the
Other Side of Your Mountain,
You Would Move It!

The Spirit of Faith

If You Knew What Was on the Other Side of Your Mountain, You Would Move It!

Mark Hankins

Mark Hankins Ministries
Alexandria, Louisiana

Unless otherwise indicated, all scriptural quotations are from the *King James Version* of the Bible.

Quotations of Smith Wigglesworth are taken from *Ever Increasing Faith*, Wayne E. Warner, ed., revised ed. (Springfield, MO: Gospel Publishing House, 1971).

Some quotations are the author's paraphrase.

The Spirit of Faith: If You Knew What Was on the Other Side of Your Mountain, You Would Move It!

Second Edition 2004

Published by
MHM Publications
P.O. Box 12863
Alexandria, LA 71315
ISBN 1-889981-06-0

Editorial Consultant: Phyllis Mackall, Broken Arrow, Oklahoma

Printed in the United States of America.

Contents

WHOSOEVER...

EVERYBODY won't.

ANYBODY can.

SOMEBODY will.

WHOSOEVER...

Introduction
If You Can Hear This...

One of my favorite stories happened during the years of the Great Depression here in the United States.

Long lines of jobless Americans were a common sight in the larger cities during the 1930's. Long periods of unemployment had caused many to lose faith in themselves and in their future. Feeling angry and humiliated, many were living on charity.

There was an employer who had one job available. As the word got out, a long line of applicants formed outside his office for an interview and a chance at employment. His secretary showed applicants into the boss' office one at a time.

During the middle of the process, one man ran from the back of the line, past the secretary, and right into the boss' office. In a few minutes, the boss came out with the man and announced to the others waiting in line that they could go home, because this man had the job.

Many began to complain that the man had not waited his turn, and it was not fair. The boss explained that during the interviewing process, he had thought of a quicker way to select the right person.

Because he needed someone who could understand Morse code, he tapped out so everyone could hear, "If you can hear this, jump up now and run into my office. You have the job." All the men and women in line heard the tapping, but it did not mean anything to them. However, it changed the life of this new employee.

Everybody — Anybody — Somebody

Faith begins with hearing a certain sound that other people cannot hear. Romans 10:17, 18 says, **"So then faith cometh by hearing, and hearing by the word of God. But I say, Have they not heard? Yes verily, their sound went into all the earth, and their words unto the end of the world."**

Everybody won't — anybody can — somebody will: That is the definition of "whosoever." Jesus continually used the word "whosoever." Jesus also said in Mark 4:23-25:

> **If any man have ears to hear, let him hear. And he said unto them, Take heed what ye hear; with what measure ye mete, it shall be measured to you: and unto you that hear shall more be given. For he that hath, to him shall be given: and he that hath not, from him shall be taken even that which he hath.**

Our *hearing* has a lot to do with our having. Some have said that there are two groups of people: the *haves* and the *have nots*. Jesus also implied that there are two groups of people: the *hearers* and the *hear nots*. (Maybe that isn't good English, but you know what I mean.)

Faith comes by hearing a certain sound. Faith comes by hearing the Word of God. The Word of God opens our ears to the supernatural plan and provision of God.

The Sound of Abundance

After 3 1/2 years of drought, the prophet Elijah said, "There is a sound of abundance of rain." Elijah began to pray on the top of Mount Carmel when there was not a cloud in sight. He prayed persistently until a cloud about the size of a man's hand appeared. Then he outran the king's chariot as the "abundance of rain" fell and brought new life to the land (1 Kings 18:41-46).

Elijah's faith began by *hearing the sound* of "abundance of rain." No one else could hear anything, but Elijah was hearing from heaven. As he prayed, his faith became sight and substance. But he got it on the inside before he got it on the outside.

The voice of the Lord is upon the people today in every nation! God is looking for people who can hear the sound of His voice and follow His plan and purpose. *This sound always brings the supernatural power of God.* This sound will get us praying like Elijah prayed. Elijah prayed with persistence and expectation. He knew it was God's will, and the manifestation must come.

There is a sound of salvation, healing, deliverance, and blessing in the Gospel of Christ.

The spirit of faith today hears, believes, and speaks the same sound. The spirit of faith can be heard and seen. Faith acts on the Word of God. Faith acts like the Bible is true. Today, the Spirit of God is saying, "If you can hear this, jump up now and run into my office. You have the job."

The spirit of faith is also a positive attitude. A person cannot be negative, critical, and constantly complaining and claim to have a spirit of faith.

I heard the story about a man who was asleep in his bedroom, and some friends played a joke on him. While he was sleeping, they wiped a piece of Limburger cheese under his nose.

Immediately, the man woke up and exclaimed, "Man, it sure stinks in here!" He walked out of his bedroom into the living room and said, "It stinks in here!" Then he walked into the kitchen and said, "It stinks in here!"

He went out the front door, looked up at the sky, breathed in deeply, and said, "The whole world stinks!"

The lesson from this story is that anytime it stinks everywhere you go, the stink is underneath your nose. You are carrying the stink with you.

Some people are negative and critical all the time and think there is something wrong with everyone else when they are the one who has the problem. A negative, critical attitude is not a spirit of faith.

You can take the Word of God and clean under your nose or clean your mind with the word of faith. As you meditate on the Word, your mind is renewed, and your attitude is changed. Then, everywhere you go, you can smell victory!

The apostle Paul said, **"Now thanks be unto God, which always causeth us to triumph in Christ, and maketh manifest the savour [smell] of his knowledge by us in every place"** (2 Corinthians 2:14). Paul faced many tough problems, but he said, "It smells like victory to me." He had a spirit of faith.

We having the same spirit of faith, according as it is written, I believed, and therefore have I spoken; we also believe, and therefore speak.

2 Corinthians 4:13

IF YOU KNEW

what was on

the other side

of your

mountain,

YOU WOULD

MOVE IT!

1

Your Mountain Needs To Hear Your Voice

"If you knew what was on the other side of your mountain, you would move it!"

These words came to me as I was praying and studying. The Holy Spirit was trying to get my attention. He began to give me a vision of the possibilities that God wanted to do in my life, but there were some "mountains" between God's best blessings and me.

Something was hindering or blocking the blessings of God in my life. God had some great, glorious, marvelous, wonderful things prepared for me that were being blocked.

To motivate me to use my faith, the Holy Spirit said again and again, "If you knew what was on the other side of your mountain, you would move it!"

As I looked at Mark 11:23 over and over again, I began to get a clearer understanding of what Jesus was saying: **"For verily I say unto you, That whosoever shall say unto this mountain, Be thou removed, and be thou cast into the sea; and shall not doubt in his**

1

heart, but shall believe that those things which he saith shall come to pass; he shall have whatsoever he saith."

There is a similar message from Jesus in Luke 17:6: **"And the Lord said, If ye had faith as a grain of mustard seed, ye might say unto this sycamine tree, Be thou plucked up by the root, and be thou planted in the sea; and it should obey you."**

Here the illustration is a "sycamine tree." Someone joked, "I have identified my problem, and I am 'sick of mine.'" Sometimes things will stay around until you get sick and tired of being sick and tired, and you determine that things must change in your life.

Here Jesus uses the illustration of a tree, because moving a tree requires dealing with some roots that have been there for a long time. The tree and its roots could represent a variety of problems in your life.

I like what Smith Wigglesworth said in the book, *Ever Increasing Faith*: "Any man may be changed by faith no matter how he may be fettered." In Mark 11:23, you can see that Jesus said that this kind of faith will work for "whosoever," and it will work on "whatsoever." This will work for anyone on anything!

Notice exactly the way that Jesus stated this in Luke 17:6: "...say unto this sycamine tree, Be thou plucked up by the root, and be thou planted in the sea; and it should obey you." Again, "It should obey you." Jesus did not say it would obey your favorite anointed preacher; it will obey you! He did not even say that it would obey God; He said, "It should obey you!"

When you put this with Mark 11:23, **"...whosoever shall say unto this mountain...he shall have whatsoever he saith,"** you can see the power of faith-filled words.

You can see that it is not up to God or someone else to deal with the situation. Your mountain will obey you! Your mountain needs to hear your voice!

Jesus did not say to talk to God about the problem; He told you to speak to the problem yourself. Your mountain needs to hear your voice. After all, it is your mountain or tree or problem, and it is in the way of supernatural increase and blessing in your life.

You may think, "I'm waiting on God," when God is really waiting on you! Often we miss it when we don't examine the scriptures closely enough.

Your mountain needs to hear your voice! You could make it personal right now and say, "My mountain needs to hear my voice!"

Your Voice Is Your Address in the Spirit

What is there about your voice that is so important? Why did Jesus say, "...he shall have whatsoever he *saith*"?

First, there is no other voice like your voice. *Your voice is your address in the realm of the spirit.* Scientists tell us that the voiceprint is just as accurate in determining an individual's identity as his fingerprint. They say there is no other voice like your voice. In certain high security situations, a person must speak, and his voice must be recognized before clearance is given.

The psalmist David said, **"In my distress I called upon the Lord, and cried unto my God: he heard my voice out of his temple, and my cry came before him, even into his ears. Then the earth shook and trembled; the foundations of the hills moved..."** (Psalm 18:6, 7).

It doesn't take long for your voice to reach heaven and enter the ears of Almighty God, who is the source of your authority as a believer. Heaven responds to your voice. If your voice moves heaven, you know it moves mountains and trees. This is the way to have a change of scenery in your life. You must lift up your voice with the voice of faith that believes, expects, and will not be denied.

E. W. Kenyon said, "The reason the majority of Christians are weak, though they are earnest, yet they are weak, is because they have never dared to make a confession of what they are in Christ."[1]

Not only does God respond to the voice of faith, but angels are also activated by your words. An angel

4

told Daniel, **"...thy words were heard, and I am come for thy words"** (Daniel 10:12). Daniel's words brought the answer from heaven, and the angel came to exactly the right address!

Ruth Ward Heflin points out in her book *Glory* that the word "ladder" in the Old Testament, when Jacob saw angels ascending and descending (Genesis 28:12), has the same numerical value as the word "voice" in the New Testament.[2]

Is it possible that angels travel on your "voice ladder"? Your voice is the highway that angels travel on to bring things to you from heaven. Traffic could be blocked right now if you are not saying much. God needs you to believe and speak. He needs you to lift your voice in faith for His power to be released at the point of your need. This is one of the reasons why you should lift your voice more in praise and faith to God.

If There Is a Mountain in Your Way, "Quark It"

Sometime ago I saw an article in *Time* magazine (February 19, 1996) that caught my attention. The article, "What's Hiding in the Quarks," tells how the discovery of quarks was made at the giant Tevatron accelerator at the Fermi National Accelerator Laboratory near Chicago.

The evidence comes from collisions between subatomic protons and antiprotons at very high speeds.

Not only were quarks discovered, but the Tevatron is so powerful, it can investigate the structure of the quarks themselves.

What are quarks made of? What is hiding in the quarks? The article states:

> Physicists were understandably over-joyed in 1994 when they discovered the top quark. At last after 17 years of searching, they had found the sixth — and, according to the theorists, the last — of matter's tiniest, most fundamental building blocks.
>
> The most troublesome loose end in the so-called Standard Model of particle physics had been tidied up.
>
> Or so they thought. According to a report in the current *Science*, the same people who discovered the top quark may have inad-vertently made a much more revolutionary discovery. Contrary to what physicists have believed for the past 30 years, quarks may not be the most basic units of matter after all.[3]

There is something smaller than the atom and the proton. All matter is made of this secret substance! The answer helps us see the origin of all things. The answer could be what many scientists believe today: Quarks are made of sound waves.

I believe this is the answer, because that is what the Bible teaches. The tiniest building block of all things is sound waves. Genesis 1:3 says, **"And God said, Let there be light: and there was light."** Over and over it says in Genesis, "And God *said.*"

Again, in Psalm 33:6, 9 we read, **"By the word of the Lord were the heavens made; and all the host of them by the breath of his mouth...For he spake, and it was done; he commanded, and it stood fast."**

You can clearly see that *God created everything with His voice.* He spoke the worlds into existence. You can also see that things created with words could also be dismantled or dissolved with words.

That is the power of Jesus' description of the God-kind of faith in Mark 11:23. The example He gave the disciples by cursing the fig tree was not a "deity trick" reserved for the Godhead. Jesus said, "Whosoever shall *say*...." Jesus always lifted man into the realm of fellowship with God.

Another biblical evidence that quarks are made of sound waves is found in Hebrews 11:3: **"Through faith we understand that the worlds were framed by the word of God, so that things which are seen were not made of things which do appear."**

The worlds were framed by the Word of God. This great faith chapter in the Bible takes us back before

7

Abraham's faith to the God-kind of faith that was used in creation. Abraham had to catch the spirit of faith before the miracle that God had promised him could be performed.

It is described in Romans 4:17: **"(As it is written, I have made thee a father of many nations,) before him whom he believed, even God, who quickeneth the dead and calleth those things which be not as though they were."**

The Words Spoken to You
Must Be Spoken Through You

God calls things which be not as though they were. *God calls things*. Abraham had to agree with God before the miracle could come to pass. The word spoken to you must be spoken *through* you.

Lilian B. Yeomans said it this way: "God has tied himself irrevocably to human cooperation in the execution of divine purposes. He has made man's faith a determining factor in the work of redemption."[4] God is looking for someone to believe Him and say the same thing.

Now we can understand Hebrews 11:1: **"Now faith is the substance of things hoped for, the evidence of things not seen."** *The Amplified Bible* says, **"Now faith is the assurance (the confirmation, the title-deed) of the things [we] hope for, being the proof of things [we]** hope for, being the proof of things [we] do not see and the conviction of their reality — faith perceiving as real fact what is not revealed to the senses."[5]

Faith is the *substance* — the substance that everything is made of is faith. The *Cotton Patch* translation says, "Now faith is the turning of dreams into deeds; it is betting your life on unseen realities."[6]

Faith always comes with a *sound*, a *voice*, and a *word*. The visible was made from the invisible. Things that are seen are not made of things that can be seen. The unseen is more powerful than the seen. That is why we walk by faith and not by sight (2 Corinthians 5:7).

Hiding in the quarks is the voice of faith that frames our world. The word of faith contains the building blocks of the will of God in our lives. All the redemptive rights and privileges that belong to us in Christ must be appropriated by faith. The authority of the believer is released through the words that move mountains and trees and make demons flee.

Whosoever Shall Have Whatsoever

Jesus said, "Whosoever...shall have whatsoever he saith" (Mark 11:23). We can draw five simple conclusions from this scripture:

1. If it was God's will for the mountain to be there, Jesus would not have told you to move it.

2. If you only knew what was on the other side of your mountain, you would move it.
3. If it is there, you can move it. There is no mountain in the sphere of your life that you cannot move.
4. Your mountain needs to hear your voice.
5. If what you have in life is all up to God, Jesus never would have said Mark 11:23.

If there is a mountain in your way, *"Quark it!"* It will obey you. God is holding you responsible to "frame your world" with His Word. The devil would like to frame your world with doubt, fear, depression, sickness, and poverty, but the Word of God will put him on the run.

Jesus told you to speak to the mountain. The mountain has been speaking to you, telling you how big it is, how long it has been there, and that it is impossible to move. Some people have actually gotten into denial about the mountain or the obstacles in their lives. They say, "There is no mountain, there is no mountain." But they are just hiding their eyes and pretending their mountain is not there.

Don't get into denial. Someone said, "De Nile is a river in Egypt." Jesus said for you to speak to the mountain, not deny its existence.

Don't talk to God about it. Talk to the mountain. Dial up the mountain. Dial 1-800-MOUNTAIN. For most people, it is a local call! Talk to your mountain directly and tell it to be removed and cast into the sea. It will be as though it had never been there! *"Quark it!"*

The LANGUAGE of REDEMPTION is the LANGUAGE of **FAITH**.

It is the language of **VICTORY**, **BLESSING**, **SALVATION**... it is the LANGUAGE OF GOD.

2
The Language of Redemption

The dictionary defines "language" as:

- The expression or communication of thoughts and feelings by means of vocal sounds.
- The particular form or manner of selecting and combining words characteristic of a person, group, etc.; form, style, or kind of expression in words; as the language of poetry.
- The particular words and phrases of a profession, group, etc., as, the language of the army.

However, the most important language in the world is the language of redemption. We must learn to understand and speak the language of the Gospel of Christ. As with any language, you must always hear it before you can speak it.

I have preached frequently in East Africa since I was 17 years old. I loved the sound of Swahili and endeavored to learn as much of it as possible when I was there.

When I first went there in 1970, many in Tanzania, now Kenya, knew English. It was known as "the *money* language." If you knew English, you were more valuable in the job market, and, therefore, you made more money than other people. It also increased your international ability. All the younger students were encouraged to learn English.

I thought "the *money* language" was an interesting phrase. The Gospel of Christ is the *salvation* language, the *healing* language, the *victory* language, and the *blessing* language.

The language of *redemption* is what happened in the death, burial, and resurrection of Christ and what He is doing for us right now, interceding for us at the right hand of the Father. We must learn what happened when Jesus took His blood into heaven and purchased our eternal redemption.

The Word of Faith

We must learn to speak the language of redemption that the apostle Paul called "the word of faith" (Romans 10:8-10). The vocabulary of salvation and the tenses make a sound that releases the power of God.

The Gospel in English, French, Swahili, Spanish, Japanese, and other languages is the power of God. The phrase "Christ *hath* redeemed us" is in the past tense, which means it has already been taken care of in Christ. He *hath* blessed us. He *hath* healed us. He *hath* delivered us. He *hath* translated us. These are all past tense.

Since He *hath*, by faith we have. *Now* faith is. In Christ, we must learn a new language — the language of God. We must speak the word of faith, "the money language" of heaven. Faith is heaven's currency.

Speak to the Rock

You will remember that in the Old Testament, when Moses struck the rock, water gushed out to supply the whole nation of Israel as they went through the wilderness. The next time they needed water, God again told Moses to speak to the rock. But Moses was angry, and he smote the rock instead.

God became angry with Moses and later refused to allow him to enter the Promised Land. Not only did Moses disobey God when he smote the rock; he destroyed the parallel between the Rock which is Christ and the picture of our redemption. The Rock Jesus was smitten *once* on the cross.

"*Once*," the Book of Hebrews says over and over again, Jesus purchased our redemption. What Jesus did once was done so well it will never have to be done again (Hebrews 9:12).

Two thousand years ago, Jesus, the Rock, was smitten. Now when you speak to the Rock, the water will freely flow. As you speak the Word of God, there is full provision for your every need. So speak to the Rock. The Promised Land is yours today!

Scientists and anthropologists are still attempting to understand creation and what man is. What makes man different from the rest of creation? We know from Genesis that man was made in the image of God. We know that man is a *spirit* being; he has a *soul*; and he lives in a *body* (1 Thessalonians 5:23).

The Gift of Gab

I recently found this interesting article, "The Gift of Gab," by Matt Cartmill in *Discover* magazine. Here are some excerpts:

> People can talk. Other animals can't. They can all communicate in one way or another but their whinnies and wiggles don't do the jobs that language does. The birds and beasts can use their signals to attract, threaten, or alert each other, but they can't ask questions, strike bargains, tell stories, or lay out a plan of action.
>
> Those skills make Homo sapiens a uniquely successful, powerful, and dangerous mammal. Other creatures' signals carry only a few limited kinds of information about what's happening at the moment, but language lets us tell each other in limitless detail about what used to be or will be or might

be...Without language, we would be only a sort of upright chimpanzee with funny feet and clever hands. With it, we are the self-possessed masters of the planet.[1]

The Power To Choose

You can see that language is unique to man. God created us eternal spirit beings in His image with the power of speech. James 3 is clear that the tongue determines our direction and destiny. We have the power to choose blessing or cursing, life or death (Deuteronomy 30:19).

The Lord Jesus said in Mark 11:23 that "whosoever shall have whatsoever he saith." Words determine the boundaries and set the limits on our lives. Jesus said, **"By thy words thou shalt be justified, and by thy words thou shalt be condemned"** (Matthew 12:37).

The Gospel is the language of faith. Believing and speaking are the two most fundamental ingredients in faith. I have heard the testimonies of two persons who died and came back from the dead. One was from Zaire, and the other was from the United States.

I thought it was interesting that both said when their spirits returned to their bodies, they entered through their mouths. God breathed the breath of life into Adam's mouth. If your spirit enters or exits your body through your mouth, why would the impact of words or speech on our lives seem strange? **"Death and life are in the power of the tongue...,"** according to Proverbs 18:21.

3
The Sound of Faith

Several years ago, I went hunting for coyote in Arizona with a friend who was an avid hunter. We got up early in the morning, while it was still dark, and put on camouflage outfits — pants, shirt, hat, and boots.

My shotgun and pistol were also camouflaged. Even my hands and face were covered with camouflage paint. My friend also gave me a pair of camouflage glasses with a camouflage veil. I was so camouflaged, when I looked in the mirror, I couldn't even see myself!

We went out on a mountainside and sat on the ground under a big bush, with camouflage netting wrapped around us. My friend then began to call the coyotes with a little wooden call he blew. It made a loud, squealing noise like the sound of a wounded rabbit. When the coyotes heard the squeal of the hurt rabbit, they would come for what they thought was a nice meal.

My friend and I stayed under the bush for several hours, calling the coyotes. I was starting to feel pretty ridiculous, because we were two grown men dressed like Rambo sitting there making crazy noises.

We never got a coyote that day, but I learned a valuable lesson. The Lord began to talk to me about faith. Many people, even Spirit-filled Christians, are continually whining and speaking defeat and depression, calling up the "coyotes" of failure. Their "wounded rabbit" call attracts the devil, and he comes to devour them for lunch! It is open season on the person who whines, complains, and constantly speaks fear and failure.

That kind of attitude opens the door to the devil. We have many "wounded rabbits" in the church who need to change their sound. I don't believe the devil can kill anyone anytime he wants. He must get you to agree with doubt and fear before he can do you any harm.

Agree With God

Faith agrees with God and shuts the door on the devil. By changing your sound to a bold declaration of who you are in Christ Jesus, you will begin to attract the blessings of God in a greater measure.

How does one change a lifelong habit of "wounded rabbit" language? A good place to begin is Philemon 6, "That the communication of thy faith may become effectual by the acknowledging of every good thing which is in you in Christ Jesus."

We need to acknowledge our identification with Christ by boldly saying, "...The Lord is my helper, and I will not fear..." (Hebrews 13:6).

I am who God says I am. I have what God says I have. I can do what God says I can do.

Many good things are in us who are in Christ. The apostle Paul says that our faith will become effective by acknowledging every good thing that is in us because we are in Christ.

We will no longer speak the cry of defeat, fear, and doubt — *but by acknowledging our identification with Christ, we will begin making the sounds of victory, health, prosperity, and blessings.*[1]

The Spirit of Faith
will make a tadpole
SLAP A WHALE.

It will make you
SWING OUT OVER
HELL ON A CORNSTALK
and spit in
the devil's eye.

4
The Spirit of Faith

We having the same spirit of faith, according as it is written, I believed and therefore have I spoken; we also believe and therefore speak.

2 Corinthians 4:13

As I meditated on this verse, I got these words: The "principles" of faith are taught, but the "spirit" of faith is caught. The "principles" of faith must be taught, but the "spirit" of faith must be caught.

Jesus spent much of His time teaching. The teaching ministry of Jesus was valuable and necessary. If people automatically knew how to receive from God and walk with Him, why did Jesus spend so much time teaching? The fact is, we must have the teaching of the Word of God.

Jesus' teaching was so plain and simple, anyone could understand exactly what He meant. He said what He meant, and He meant what He said. His illustrations are so clear, you would need a theologian to misunderstand them!

Catch the Spirit of Faith and Pass It On

The great thing about Jesus is that He will stay with you until you understand it. However, there is more to faith than "principles." Paul said, "We having the same spirit of faith..." (2 Corinthians 4:13). You must catch the "spirit of faith." The spirit of faith must be imparted. You can catch it by associating with people who have it.

The spirit of faith is contagious! When you have it, you pass it on to others. Abraham passed it on to his children and grandchildren. Joshua caught it from Moses. Elisha caught it from Elijah and doubled it. David's mighty men in the cave of Adullam were not so mighty until they caught the spirit of faith from David.

The disciples caught it from Jesus. Timothy caught it from Paul. These are just a few examples in the Word of God. Many are still catching the spirit of faith today. Even if you already have it, you can have more and double it, as Elisha did.

Faith Has No Limits

The spirit of faith is unlimited. Jesus said in Mark 9:23, **"...If thou canst believe, all things are possible to him that believeth."** The spirit of faith takes the limits off God. God is not only a big, big, big God; He is a good, good, good God!

Take the limits off His ability and His goodness. God can do and wants to do things for you that are so glorious, there will be no doubt that He did it. I have found that God is so good, He will do things for you that you wouldn't do for yourself.

The spirit of faith believes and speaks the unlimited possibilities of God. **"For with God nothing shall be impossible"** (Luke 1:37).

The spirit of faith will make a tadpole slap a whale. It will make you swing out over hell on a cornstalk and spit in the devil's eye. You can never *achieve* the impossible if you never *attempt* the impossible. The spirit of faith will position you to possess God's best blessings.

You Are One Step Away From a Miracle

Some time ago, I was watching a nationally televised NCAA football game. The team was ranked in the top ten in the country, and the quarterback was one of the best in college football. The play had been called in the huddle, and the players were lined up at the line of scrimmage to run the play.

The quarterback came up to the line, began to yell out the numbers, and bent over to receive the snap of the ball before realizing that he was behind the guard instead of the center.

If you know anything about American football, you know the center is the one who snaps the ball to the quarterback, not the guard. In the middle of his calling the play, he took one step over right behind the center, and hollered, "Hut, hut, hut." The ball was hiked to him, and the play was run successfully.

I laughed a little while I was watching this. Then the Lord spoke to me, using that illustration. He said, "Some people need to make a small adjustment if they are going to receive from Me. Some people are only one step away from a miracle!"

It isn't far from the guard to the center. Some people look like they are lined up with the Word of God, and they sound like they are ready to run the play, but really there is a small adjustment that must be made before things work right. It isn't difficult, but it requires humbling yourself and moving into a closer agreement with God's ways, power, and plan. Sometimes, it is just one small step over to receive from God.

Believe It and Say It

The spirit of faith works by believing and speaking. The spirit of faith requires your "speaker" to be hooked up to your "believer." In other words, for faith to work properly, it must be in your heart and in your mouth (Romans 10:8-10; Mark 11:23).

The word spoken to you must be spoken *through* you. The apostle Paul illustrated this in the middle of a life-threatening storm at sea. The spirit of faith does not guarantee that you won't have any storms in life. The storms of life come to everyone. However, the spirit of faith is what enables you to face the storms and overcome.

The spirit of faith will put you over instead of your going under. Paul told his shipmates, **"Wherefore, sirs, be of good cheer: for I believe God, that it shall be even as it was told me"** (Acts 27:25). In the middle of trouble, Paul said, "Cheer up, everyone! I believe God."

One person with the spirit of faith can change the destinies of many others. Paul said, "It shall be even as it was told me." God's Word is the foundation for our faith. The spirit of faith believes and speaks. What does the Word say? What has God spoken to you? Believe it and say it. It will put you over. It will take you through the storms of life and enable you to finish your course.

When Faith Cometh, You Knoweth

"So then faith cometh by hearing, and hearing by the word of God" (Romans 10:17). When faith cometh, you knoweth! Maybe that's not good English, but you get the message. It is no great secret where faith comes from. Faith is the by-product of the Word of God. Notice it says by "hearing and hearing" the Word of God.

Sometimes we don't understand it the first time around, so God will repeat it. Has God ever told you anything more than once? He has told me some things many times. Some times He will say the same thing exactly, and sometimes He will use someone to say it a little differently so I can understand it. The Word of God is faith food.

When Faith Cometh, Fear Goeth

When faith cometh, fear goeth! Fear leaveth when faith cometh. God is a faith God (Hebrews 11:6). God works by faith. The devil is a fear devil. The devil works by fear. There are 365 times in the Bible where we are told "fear not." Jesus said, **"Fear not: believe only"** (Luke 8:50).

The apostle Paul, writing in Second Corinthians 4:13, says, **"We having the same spirit of faith, according as it is written, I believed, and therefore have I spoken; we also believe, and therefore speak."** He quotes the psalmist David, **"I believed, therefore have I spoken..."** (Psalm 116:10).

There can be no doubt that David had a spirit of faith. He killed a lion, a bear, the giant Goliath, and more than 10,000 Philistines. Case closed — the man had a spirit of faith.

However, in the Psalms, we see David dealing with an overcoming fear. One of my favorites is Psalm 27:1, **"The Lord is my light and my salvation; whom shall I fear? The Lord is the strength of my life; of whom shall**

I be afraid?" Here we see David believing and speaking. The spirit of faith requires both.

Faith Determines Your Destiny

In the midst of adversity, David was overcoming fear. The spirit of faith is necessary to do the will of God. The Bible says, **"Without faith it is impossible to please him: for he that cometh to God must believe that he is, and that he is a rewarder of them that diligently seek him"** (Hebrews 11:6). Faith is absolutely necessary to please God and do the will of God.

Lilian B. Yeomans said, "God has tied Himself irrevocably to human cooperation in the execution of divine purposes. He has made man's faith a determining factor in the work of redemption."[1]

Although He is sovereign, God has tied Himself to human cooperation to work out His divine purposes. Jesus said, **"...According to your faith be it unto you"** (Matthew 9:29).

As you know, the first ingredient in the spirit of faith is to believe. In Mark 5, when the woman with the issue of blood touched Jesus, she got healed. Jesus said, **"Daughter, your faith has made you whole."** Brother Kenneth E. Hagin said the Lord told him, "If her faith made her whole, then your faith will make you whole."

Fear Not, Only Believe

At the time, Jesus was on the way to the house of Jairus, the ruler of the synagogue, to pray for his daughter, who was dying.

When Jesus told the woman, "Your faith has made you whole," Jairus' servants came from his house, saying, "Don't trouble Jesus any longer. Your daughter is already dead." When Jesus heard them say that to Jairus, He gave him some vital information: "Fear not, only believe."

There is a fight to faith. At that moment, Jairus could choose whether he would believe the bad report, get in fear, and give up on his miracle. But Jesus said, "Let Me tell you what to do in this situation: Fear not, only believe."

When the doctors told us that my wife, Trina, had a brain tumor, all the specialists and neurosurgeons gave their opinions and bad reports for seven days. Friends called and asked, "What are you going to do?"

All I said was, "I don't know what I'm going to do, but I know what I'm not going to do." I decided to resist the spirit of fear and "fear not." That means I remained in faith and continued to believe. I believe God. I believe the Word of God. I choose to fear not, only believe. Believing is a choice.

Fear has several relatives and companions: doubt, anxiety, stress, and worry. All stem from the same fear.

It is impossible to have a spirit of faith and a spirit of fear at the same time. When you have a spirit of faith, you don't have a spirit of fear.

The Bible says that in the last days, people's hearts will fail them because of fear (Luke 21:26). In Second Timothy 1:7, Paul writes, **"For God hath not given us a spirit of fear; but of power, and of love, and of a sound mind."** If God didn't give you a spirit of fear, where did you get it?

Fear comes from the devil. The devil is a fear devil. God is a faith God. Jesus said in Mark 9:23, **"...If thou canst believe, all things are possible to him that believeth."** This means, "Fear not, only believe."

You Choose Faith or Fear

Not only do you believe, but you also have to say what you believe. There will be a fight in the worst of your circumstances. There will be a moment when you must choose to either believe God or be full of fear. You have a choice to make at that point.

Jesus grabbed Jairus right in the middle of his choice and gave him a word. Jesus will give you a word right in the middle of your crisis, too. He knows what others are telling you; He knows the doubts that are flooding your mind and the way the devil is attacking you. Jesus hears and says, "I'd like to interrupt the fear and doubt and give you a word from heaven: Fear not, only believe."

Jairus might have told Jesus, "I don't know what is going on. I don't know how all this happened; but if you told me to fear not and believe only, that is where my responsibility ends. That is all I have to do, and I'll let You take care of the rest."

You don't have to change the whole situation. You only have to do your part, and your part is to fear not, only believe. Jesus said, "If you can stay in faith, I'll come to your house. I'll bring my faith friends — Peter, James, and John."

Jairus' relatives and friends were already planning his daughter's funeral, but Jesus told them, "Get out! It's not over. She's not dead; she's just sleeping."

When the devil says it is all over, Jesus says it is not all over; it has just been delayed for a little while.

Would you like Jesus to visit your house, bring some of His disciples, and throw out doubt, fear, confusion, stress, and anxiety — and breathe new life into dead things? Jesus said to fear not, only believe. When you have a spirit of faith, you say what you believe.

God can take care of you. He can work in your life and undo everything the devil has done. God has power. He has angels on assignment to watch over you. He is able to raise the dead, heal the sick, cast out devils, and turn your whole life around. When He speaks, faith comes. And when faith comes, fear goes!

Deal With Fear Supernaturally

There is a fight to faith. You cannot deal with fear naturally. You cannot reason with fear. Fear is a spirit; a supernatural problem. You have to have a word from God — the word of faith.

Romans 10:17 says, **"So then faith cometh by hearing, and hearing by the word of God."** When faith comes, healing comes, blessing comes, joy comes, and fear goes. When faith comes, you know. Faith is the substance of things hoped for, the evidence of things not seen. When faith comes, the substance comes, and you know you have it.

The devil would like to starve your faith. Smith Wigglesworth said, "Some people feed their bodies three hot meals a day, and their spirits one cold snack a week, and wonder why they're weak in faith."

You must feed on the Word of God to be strong in faith. Hear it, meditate on it, speak it, and go over and over it until you feel the substance of faith rise up in your spirit. Faith cometh!

Close the Door on the Devil

There are more than 100 different kinds of fear. These fears can be irrational, but since fear is of the devil, it does not have to be rational. Here is a list of some of the phobias that plague mankind:

Acrophobia: fear of heights

Claustrophobia: fear of enclosed places

Agoraphobia: fear of outdoors and open spaces (affects 2 million Americans)

Anthropophobia: fear of people

Cynophobia: fear of dogs

Kleptophobia: fear of thieves

Aquaphobia: fear of water

Brontophobia: fear of thunderstorms

Dentophobia: fear of dentists

Skiaphobia: fear of shadows

Cardiophobia: fear of heart disease

Triskaidekaphobia: fear of the number 13

Arachibutyrophobia: fear of getting peanut butter stuck to the roof of the mouth

Amaxophobia: fear of riding in vehicles

Anuptaphobia: fear of staying single

Hematophobia: fear of the sight of blood

Peniaphobia: fear of poverty

Tropophobia: fear of changes

Gephyrophobia: fear of crossing bridges

Pantaphobia: the morbid dread of everything

There are too many phobias to list. Psychologists say that *thanatophobia*, the fear of death, is the root of all fears. If you have a spirit of fear, you did not get it from God.

Fear opens the door to the devil, and fear is connected to lack of power, lack of love, and mental problems. The spirit of fear must be dealt with supernaturally.

The Word of God breaks the spirit of fear. Faith comes by hearing, and hearing by the Word of God. When faith comes, fear goes. There is faith, power, love, and mental soundness in the Word of God.

Hebrews 2:14, 15 says that Jesus, through death, destroyed the power of the devil and delivered those who through fear of death were subject to its bondage during all their lifetimes. Jesus has delivered us from the power and the control of the devil!

David wrote, **"I sought the Lord, and he heard me, and delivered me from all my fears"** (Psalm 34:4). David had a spirit of faith, but he still had to overcome the enemy of fear. Fear not only opens the door to the devil; it will also paralyze you from moving with God's plan for your life.

The Voice of Faith

You can be free from all your fears. When faith comes, fear goes. Do not cast away your confidence. Faith in God is faith in His Word. Believe God, believe the Word, and speak with the voice of faith. Your faith is voice-activated.

Sometimes you must get radical when you deal with fear, doubt, and anxiety. Fear is a spirit, and it will come against your mind. You must deal with it by saying, "You foul spirit of fear, I resist you in the name of Jesus. I refuse to doubt. I fear not; I only believe. I made that choice. Now get out!"

When the supernatural comes into contact with the natural, something has to give! When the power of God is in manifestation, it will hit you on the top of your head, go down your back, and get in your legs. You will say, "It's all over me, and it's keeping me alive. I shall not die, but I shall live and declare the works of God."

We know that with faith you always get it on the inside before you get it on the outside. There is a fight of faith necessary to lay hold of the blessings of God. Get a grip on the spirit of faith — catch it and keep it!

5
The Fight of Faith

One of Abraham Lincoln's favorite stories was about one of his neighbors who had a little dog that could whip all the big dogs.

When someone asked the man how his little dog could whip all the big dogs, he said, "Your big dog is not really ready to fight until the fight is half over. My little dog stays mad!"

Don't wait any longer before you really use your faith to lay hold of what belongs to you. Right now, set your goals of prayer, faith, and blessing for your life and "stay mad." Keep your faith focused all the time. Refuse to give in one inch to the devil, defeat, or discouragement.

Are you really ready to fight? First Timothy 6:12 says, **"Fight the good fight of faith, lay hold on eternal life, whereunto thou art also called and hast professed a good profession before many witnesses."**

The faith fight is the only fight believers are called to fight. We are not called to fight other people. We really are not called to fight the devil, because he is a defeated foe. Jesus defeated him 2,000 years ago.

One of Satan's strategies is to entice the believer out of the arena of faith and into the arena of feelings, sight, or circumstances. You must stay in the arena of faith, because that is where the victory is won.

Another strategy of the devil is discouragement. During the Korean War, a company of American soldiers took a particular hill in Korea 13 times and lost it every time. However, on the fourteenth attempt, they took the hill and kept it.

You may experience setbacks and delays in your life, but your faith fight is a good fight, because you win!

Never Run at Your Giant With Your Mouth Shut

Don't let the devil shut your mouth. When the devil talks trash to you, talk it right back to him. He'll try to intimidate you, just like Goliath talked to David. Do you know what David did? He started talking back to Goliath. He said, "I'm going to kill you, cut your head off, hang it in my tent, and feed your body to the birds!"

All of us have giants or things that seem bigger than we are. That's why everyone needs at least one Goliath head hanging in his tent! Some people may think that's stupid, but if you've ever fought a Goliath, you'll want to keep the head in your trophy room, too.

David activated the covenant with his confession and actions. You can do the same thing. The Lord once said to me, "Never run at your giant with your mouth shut." Often people run to see what happens, but faith always declares the outcome before the fight ever starts.

In other words, the battle is won on the *inside* before you ever win it on the *outside*. Faith declares the outcome before the battle ever starts.

Sometimes in the middle of the storm you need to say, "Hold it! I'd like to say a few things before this is over." Anyone can say things after the storm is over. Often people will say afterwards, "I just knew everything was going to turn out all right." Why didn't they say that in the middle of the struggle?

In the middle of the battle you should say, "The victory is mine." The Lord said it to me this way: "The word spoken to you must be spoken *through* you." In the midst of the storm at sea, Paul said, "I believe God. It shall be as He said."

Let me tell you who He is. Jesus said, "I am he that liveth, and was dead: and, behold, I am alive for ever more..." (Revelation 1:18). I get my words from Him — the One who went through the cross, death, hell, and the grave, and was raised from the dead. I believe God. It shall be as He told me.

The Good Fight of Faith

If you are in a faith fight now, the devil is going to make sure it's not easy for you. He's going to try to stop it. He will put roadblocks, mountains, difficulties, and hindrances everywhere he can and tell you that God is not faithful and the Word doesn't work.

You've got to say, "This is a good fight. It's not a bad fight. I am fighting the good fight of faith. I've got a good confession, and I'm going to enjoy the fight."

There is a fight to faith — a good fight and a winning fight. The "good" faith fight requires a "good" profession or confession. You must say what you believe to lay hold or possess your victory. Sometimes it is much easier to say how you feel or how things look than to say what you believe.

Paul said in Second Corinthians 4:13, **"We having the same spirit of faith...believe and...speak."**

Your faith will never rise above your confession. E. W. Kenyon said, "Confession builds the road over which faith hauls its mighty cargo."[1] If your faith is going to get some thing to your house, how would it get there? You will have to build a road or street there.

Your confession of faith should be strong enough for some eighteen-wheelers to carry heaven's cargo to your address. *Confession always precedes possession.*

If you wonder why only a few things get to your house, perhaps you have built only a narrow path with your words, and you have never taken the time to build an adequate road. If you want to change the road from being a muddy little path with potholes and trees across the way, change your confession!

Sometimes there may be what seems like a delay, but how many years did you spend confessing a footpath? Recently the State of Louisiana completed I-49 from the southern part of the state to the northern part. Even with modern technology and equipment, it took 20 years from start to finish! They started out marking the path, and for years they moved dirt and then finally poured the concrete.

It takes time to build a superhighway. So if you are expecting some major traffic to come to your house, start building the road right now! Remember, confession is the road over which faith carries its mighty cargo.

Although confession builds the road, it will never take the place of prayer. Your confession is born out of rich fellowship with the Father God. I don't mean a superficial relationship, but a heart relationship with the Father, where your spirit is in fellowship with the Lord Jesus. Your confession is born out of that fellowship.

Your words will either complete your faith, or they will defeat your faith. You must boldly confess your redemption in Christ and who you are in Him.

Who You Are in Christ

One of the biggest enemies to faith is a lack of understanding your redemption in Christ. Once you know the truth about redemption, you will enjoy the freedom Jesus purchased for you. Christ has redeemed us, according to Galatians 3:13.

Another enemy to faith is a lack of understanding who you are in Christ. You are well able to possess the land because of your union with Christ. In Him you are redeemed. In Him you are strong. In Him you are blessed. In Him you are forgiven. In Him you are always triumphant!

You must maintain a good confession of who you are in Christ to fight the good fight of faith. You must say, "I am who God says I am. I have what God says I have. I can do what God says I can do."

You can "stay mad" by realizing that Jesus paid too high a price for your freedom for you to remain bound. He paid too high a price for your healing for you to stay sick. He paid too high a price for your prosperity for you to be poor. Jesus purchased your freedom with His own blood (Hebrews 9:12)!

Your Faith Grows Exceedingly

Paul said to the church of Thessalonica, "**...when ye received the word of God which ye heard of us, ye received it not as the word of men, but as it is in truth,** the word of God..." (1 Thessalonians 2:13). That is God speaking personally and directly to you. And He said in Second Thessalonians 1:3, **"...your faith groweth exceedingly...."**

Once you believe God is talking to you, you will begin to rejoice like you have what you need now. Sometimes when you are at home and the devil comes against your mind through your feelings or circumstances, you must say, "I live by faith. I walk by faith. I believe that God is talking to me right now, so I'm going to rejoice. Victory is mine! Healing is mine! Prosperity is mine! I receive it by faith."

God Performs Things for You

In the midst of his difficulties, Job said, **"For he performeth the thing that is appointed for me; and many such things are with him"** (Job 23:14).

When you read the last chapter of Job, you will find that the Lord gave him twice as much as he had before. Theologians tell us that Job's trials, as related in the Book of Job, lasted less than a year.

Satan is the god of this world. Jesus said, **"...In the world ye shall have tribulation [difficulty]: but be of good cheer; I have overcome the world"** (John 16:33). You are not exempt from challenges, but once you know who you are in Christ and Christ is in you, you always overcome. You always come out on top.

The Lord said it to me this way: "You will have challenges in life, but you are not the *challenger*; you are the *champion*." The champion enters the ring with a different attitude from the challenger. The challenger is trying to get something. The champion, on the other hand, says, "I've got something."

God's Ability and Our Responsibility

The spirit of faith actually has two sides — ours and God's. God's ability and our responsibility are the two parts of faith. What is our response to God's ability? Grace is God's grip on you, and *faith* is your grip on God.

You study faith, you walk by faith, and you live by faith, but there are times when it may seem like your faith doesn't have the grip you need. When you sense that, look to the grace of God. Realize that God's grip on you is stronger than your grip on Him!

Even when it seems like your faith is not working, God still has hold of you. The apostle Paul said, **"Not as though I had already attained, either were already perfect..."** (Philippians 3:12). Another translation says, **"I have not gotten hold of what has gotten hold of me."**

God performs what He has spoken concerning you. Another aspect of faith is that you don't have to bring it to pass; God brings it to pass.

Brother Kenneth E. Hagin says, "You don't have to make it happen; you let it happen." That is why the person who believes has entered into rest (Hebrews 4:3). You cease from your efforts and finally, when you enter into rest, God brings it to pass.

The Bible says that the Lord gives his beloved sleep or rest (Psalm 127:2). God brings it to pass even while you are resting. He performs the things that are appointed to you. Philippians 2:13 says, **"For it is God which worketh in you both to will and to do of his good pleasure."** God has good things planned for you.

The End of Your Faith

Don't fight with your reasoning or your flesh. Don't try to figure everything out. Just say, "I'm going to rest and enjoy. The fight of faith is a good fight."

Some people think they are fighting the fight of faith, but you can tell by their face that even though they may be fighting, they are not fighting the faith fight. They are trying so hard to bring it to pass, they are getting in God's way! When you don't have a spirit of faith, everyone can see what you are going through by your countenance.

Have you ever believed God for something and gotten stuck right in the middle? You have seen the blessing to a degree, and you know there is more ahead, but it seems like you are stuck in the middle.

Peter says, "Let me show you how to get from the believing to the end." Where is the end of your faith? It is when the thing you believe for shows up, and you don't have to believe for it anymore.

To get from believing to receiving — when you have a spirit of faith — you must rejoice with **"joy unspeakable and full of glory"** (1 Peter 1:8, 9). Your faith has an end. This situation you are in has an end! The *Amplified Bible* says, **"...receiving the outcome of your faith."**[2]

When you start rejoicing, the glory of God shows up. Then you can laugh, jump, shout, and rejoice because you have seen the outcome of your faith.

6
Move to Montana

Jesus made one of the most amazing statements in the Bible in Mark 9:23, when He said, **"...If thou canst believe, all things are possible to him that believeth."** With that one statement, Jesus opened the door to the supernatural! He was encouraging us to take the limits off our lives and enter the realm of God.

We know that with God all things are possible, but Jesus put the believer in the realm of God. We know from Hebrews 11:6 that without faith it is impossible to please God. Faith pleases God and releases His supernatural ability. Unbelief and doubt limit God and stop His power. Faith takes off the limits!

At one time the State of Montana removed speed limits from its highways. I would love to spend some time driving in a state that has no speed limits! This is not the law in Montana now, however, the Autobahn in Germany has no speed limits.

During this time a newspaper article reported that a Montana highway patrolman stopped a man for going more than 100 miles per hour. However, after observing the quality of the man's vehicle and checking his driving record, the patrolman let him off without a ticket. What a place to visit — a place with no limits!

God has given us a quality vehicle in His Word to go beyond the limits of the natural man into the supernatural. Spiritually speaking, some people have never been to "Montana"; some people have only visited there once or twice; and others have decided to move there!

Learn to live every day where all things are possible. Someone said that a miracle comes your way every day. Learn to recognize the possibilities of God that surround you. Some people are content to putter through life and simply make their mortgage payments. Others reach out for the impossible and see the supernatural!

Norman Vincent Peale said, "It seems there is an invisible reservoir of abundance in the universe that can be tapped by obeying certain spiritual laws."

I like the way he said that. There is an unseen reservoir of abundance in the universe. I read that many years ago and never forgot it. There is no need to be in lack if you learn how to tap into that reservoir! As you learn the laws of God and what pleases Him, abundance will flow to you.

The Law of Faith

There are a number of universal laws. The one we will discuss here is what the apostle Paul called "the law of faith" (Romans 3:27). God is a faith God. The more we understand about faith, the better we will understand what moves Him.

God demands faith of us. Without faith it is impossible to please Him. Smith Wigglesworth said that God would pass over a million people just to find someone who believes Him.

Faith pleased God in the Old Testament. That is how Abraham received from God and became "the Father of faith." We also see Jesus in the gospels telling the woman with the issue of blood, **"Daughter, thy faith hath made thee whole..."** (Mark 5:34). Faith not only pleased Him; it seems He was looking for it. He told the Roman centurion, **"...I have not found so great faith, no, not in Israel"** (Matthew 8:10).

In the Book of Acts, we find that faith also pleases and moves the Holy Spirit. For example, in Acts 10:19, 20, the Holy Spirit told Peter to go to Caesarea with Cornelius' servants, "doubting nothing." The Holy Spirit was trying to get Peter to take the limits off God.

It takes faith to please God. God the Father, God the Son, and God the Holy Spirit are pleased by faith. Faith pleased God in both the Old and New Testaments.

In Malachi 3:6, God said, **"I am the Lord, I change not..."** Faith will please God throughout eternity. Therefore, this "law of faith" is not a temporary law; it is part of the nature of God, and it will last forever.

Mountain-Moving Faith

Learn how to walk by faith. God not only tells us how to get faith; He tells us how faith works. Jesus said in Mark 11:22, 23:

> **...Have faith in God. For verily I say unto you, That whosoever shall say unto this mountain, Be thou removed, and be thou cast into the sea; and shall not doubt in his heart, but shall believe that those things which he saith shall come to pass; he shall have whatsoever he saith.**

A note in the margin of my Bible indicates that the literal Greek meaning of verse 22 is, "Have the faith of God." If the Lord Jesus said we are to "have" the faith of God, it must be possible to "have" faith. And not only is it possible; it is necessary and mandatory.

Jesus was saying here in Mark 11 that there will be times in your life when nothing *natural* will move the mountain you are facing. It will take the *supernatural* to move that mountain. It will take the faith of God to open the door to the supernatural and release the power of God.

The God-kind of faith is an absolute necessity in this life; it is not an accessory or an option. If Jesus said to "have" faith, we must need it.

We Have the Same Spirit of Faith

This kind of faith works by believing in your heart and saying with your mouth. Writing under the inspiration of the Holy Spirit to the church at Corinth, the apostle Paul said, **"We having the same spirit of faith, according as it is written, I believed, and therefore have I spoken; we also believe, and therefore speak"** (2 Corinthians 4:13).

Paul said "we" have the same spirit of faith: "I have and you have — *we have* — the same spirit of faith. We believe and we speak. This is how faith works, by believing and speaking." Notice Paul did not say, "We are trying to get it"; he said, "We've got it!"

In Romans 12:3, Paul says that God has dealt to every man "the measure of faith." Every born-again believer has a measure of the God-kind of faith. You have a measure of mountain-moving faith! Your faith can grow and increase by feeding on the Word of God and by exercising it, because we have the same spirit of faith.

Remember, Jesus was not performing a "deity trick" in His teaching in Mark 11. He was not showing off what God could do. If He had, He never would have said,

"Whosoever shall say..." This will work for anyone. This is the law of faith that taps into God's reservoir of power and abundance to meet every need of mankind. Thank God for His Word!

Move to "Montana" in your faith. You have a measure of the God-kind of faith, and all things are possible to you, a believer!

7

Faith Ain't Pretty

A local tire store advertises in the newspaper and on television with this ad: "Hello, neighbor! Tires ain't pretty, but everyone needs tires, so you might as well get them from us at the best price." That TV ad caught my attention.

Some time later I was in a radical, wild church service where people were laughing, rejoicing, shouting, and praising God. Some were even leaping for joy, running, and dancing!

During all of this, the Lord spoke to me in this way: "Hello, neighbor! Faith ain't pretty, but everyone needs faith! So get your faith from God and learn how to release your faith and respond to the Word and the power of God."

Romans 10:17 says, **"So then faith cometh by hearing, and hearing by the word of God."** Psalm 119:162 says, **"I rejoice at thy word, as one that findeth great spoil."** Jeremiah 15:16 says, **"Thy words were found, and I did eat them; and thy word was unto me the joy and rejoicing of mine heart...."**

First Peter 1:8, 9 says, **"...yet *believing*, ye rejoice with joy unspeakable and full of glory: *Receiving* the end of your faith, even the salvation of your souls."** Notice that between "believing" and "receiving" in these verses is "joy unspeakable."

Joy Unspeakable

When you are really Bible-believing Christians, there must be some rejoicing with joy unspeakable. If the joy is "unspeakable," you must let it out somehow through laughing, shouting for joy, and leaping or dancing for joy. This kind of joy is full of glory.

The spirit of faith declares the outcome even in the middle of adversity. You see the victorious end of the challenge you are facing.

Some people would have great faith, but they are too concerned about being "pretty" all the time. They want to look "cool" or sophisticated. Real Bible faith ain't always pretty. (I know that may not be good English, but it is still true.)

Shouting, Dancing, and Running

When the glory of God is manifested, it brings the supernatural power of God.

The spirit of faith will cause you to shout while the walls are still standing, like God's people did at Jericho before the walls came down (Joshua 6:20).

54

The spirit of faith will cause you to dance like David did when the Ark of the Covenant was returned to Jerusalem and the glory returned (2 Samuel 6:14,15).

The spirit of faith may cause you to run like Elijah did when the hand of the Lord came upon him (1 Kings 18:46). The rain he had prayed and contended for was coming, and he outran the king's chariot.

The spirit of faith will cause you to sing and praise God loudly, as Paul and Silas did at midnight when they were imprisoned in chains (Acts 16:25). The power of God shook the prison and set them free.

These are demonstrations of the power of God, and they are all connected to faith. Everyone needs faith. **"...The just shall live by faith,"** Romans 1:17 says. Faith pleases God, according to Hebrews 11:6.

Lilian B. Yeomans said it this way: "God delights in his children stepping out over the aching void with nothing under their feet but the Word of God."[1] God watches as we demonstrate a faith that acts on the Word.

Often the spirit of faith may cause a person to look foolish, as Naaman did when the prophet Elisha told him to dip seven times in the muddy Jordan River (2 Kings 5:14). What God required of Naaman for his healing from leprosy was not difficult, but it seemed too foolish. Naaman's reasoning almost made him miss his miracle, but he finally acted on the prophet's word and was totally healed.

"But God hath chosen the foolish things of the world to confound the wise; and God hath chosen the weak things of the world to confound the things which are mighty" (1 Corinthians 1:27). The answer still is, **"...Not by might, nor by power, but by my spirit, saith the Lord of hosts"** (Zechariah 4:6).

Wigglesworth said that in Romans 4:17, we read of Abraham:

"(...I have made thee a father of many nations,) before him whom he believed, even God, who quickeneth the dead, and calleth those things which be not as though they were."

God help us to understand this! It is time people knew how to shout in faith as they contemplate the eternal power of our God, to whom it is nothing to quicken and raise the dead.

I come across some people who would be giants in the power of God, but they have no shout of faith. I find everywhere people who fail, even when they are praying, simply because they are just breathing sentences without uttering speech — and you cannot get victory that way.

You must learn to take the victory and shout in the face of the devil, "It is done!" Things will be different, and tremendous things will happen.

Get "Ugly" for Jesus

Recently I was ministering at a campmeeting with several other ministers. One night, the meeting became particularly radical and unusual. As people were rejoicing and enjoying the presence of God, some looked rather comical.

A minister friend of mine said to me, "Those people are not ashamed to get 'ugly' for Jesus!" I laughed and agreed. We rejoiced as people received from God.

Sometimes you have to get "ugly" for Jesus. If you want the anointing and the power of God, you must act like the Bible is true!

The spirit of faith can be seen and heard. Smith Wigglesworth said, "No man can doubt when he learns to shout."

Changed by Faith

You don't have to be perfect to have a spirit of faith. Some people disqualify themselves from the blessings of God or from being used by God because they think they have too many flaws.

While it is true that you are to keep growing spiritually, you do not need to have reached perfection to have a spirit of faith.

The great faith chapter of Hebrews 11 includes many people who were far from perfect. There were flaws in Abraham, Sarah, Noah, Moses, Samson, David, and many others in the Bible who had a spirit of faith.

I am glad that God works with imperfect people. The spirit of faith enables you to overcome in every area of your life.

Smith Wigglesworth said, "Any man may be changed by faith, no matter how he may be fettered."

Recently I was talking to a jeweler about diamonds. He said that all diamonds have a flaw somewhere that can be seen by the trained eye using a magnifying glass. However, the fake diamonds we call cubic zirconiums (cz's) are flawless. They are man-made. Although they look like diamonds, they are much cheaper, and they have only a fraction of the value of a real diamond.

Sometimes the devil will tell you that you are not the real thing, because you have a flaw. I'm sure you do have a flaw, but you are still a real diamond. At least you are not a cubic zirconium!

You are valuable to God. He sees you in Christ. He will keep working with you if you keep a spirit of faith and seek Him with all your heart. You don't have to be perfect to have a spirit of faith.

The spirit of faith comes in all sizes, colors, and ages. The spirit of faith cannot tell what color your skin is or how much education you have. The spirit of faith cannot tell whether you are handsome or homely.

The spirit of faith comes to all ages. You could be 17, like David was when he killed Goliath, or 80, like Joshua and Caleb were when they entered the Promised Land.

The spirit of faith has one thing in common — it believes and speaks. The spirit of faith acts on the Word of God.

Believe and Speak

All scripture is inspired by God (2 Timothy 3:16). The word "inspired" means "God-breathed." Jesus said in Matthew 4:4, **"...Man shall not live by bread alone, but by every word that proceedeth out of the mouth of God."**

The Word of God was spoken before it was written. It proceeded out of the mouth of God. Then it was spoken and written by men for us. It was spoken before it was written, and it was written that it might be spoken. The spirit of faith must believe and speak.

The Word of God in your mouth is God giving you mouth-to-mouth resuscitation. The spoken word gives the life of God to all who believe and speak.

8

Jesus Saw Their Faith

"Now faith is...." That's one of the great secrets of faith. Now faith is. God is looking for faith, and He can see when someone gets in the now. Jesus never told anyone to return the next day or in 30 days.

In other words, the question is not God's ability. The question is: Can you bring your faith into the now? Can you get it on the inside of you in the now — today?

This is the day, now is the time, this is the place, and you are the person! You must say, "I believe I have it now." *Once you get into the now, all things are possible with God.* Remember: Jesus never told anyone to return the next day.

Faith can be heard, and faith can be seen. If you had passed the woman with the issue of blood in the street, you would have heard her faith. She confessed, **"...If I may touch but his clothes, I shall be whole"** (Mark 6:28).

You would also have seen her faith, because she would have been moving the best way she could in her weakened, bleeding condition. Her faith caused her to be moving!

She could have just stood there and said, "If the Lord wants me to be healed, He'll just have to come to my house." But the Bible says that when she heard of Jesus, she started moving and talking or confessing.

You've got to start moving and talking, too. You've got to do something that seems impossible, and you've got to start declaring or confessing something that seems impossible — something no one but God could do for you.

What kind of a prayer line would we have in meetings today if everyone was like her, and they had already been confessing before prayer, "I know as soon as hands are laid on me, I will receive my healing! I believe I have received my healing! I know it's mine!"

Corporate Faith

You can see *individual* faith like that possessed by the woman with the issue of blood, and you can also see *corporate* faith in the gospels. Luke 5:20 says, **"When Jesus saw *their* faith...."** "Their faith" was people joining their faith together.

The four men who carried their paralyzed friend to Jesus had corporate faith, but the paralyzed man had individual faith, too.

Few invalids would have allowed themselves to be carried out of their home as he did, because it was so painful. However, this invalid allowed his friends to take him to the house where Jesus was teaching — but when they got there, they found that the house was filled with people.

I believe all of them agreed, "Let's go up on the roof. This is it. Today's the day. We're not going home. We're not coming back another day, and we're not going to see if they can make room for us. We're going up on that roof and knocking a hole in it!

Permanent Jubilee

In Luke 4, Jesus gave His sermon from Isaiah 61 — His sermon on Jubilee. Jesus was trying to bring Jubilee to Nazareth. He is always trying to bring Jubilee. He's the permanent Jubilee!

Jesus always brings healing and deliverance. He endeavors to bless you and give you victory. If you have been held hostage or were in bondage, Jesus wants to set you free.

Jesus was from Nazareth, where He was known as the son of a carpenter. He read Isaiah 61: "The Spirit of the Lord is upon me. He has anointed me. This is it. I'm the person. Now is the time. What are you going to do about it?"

The people of Nazareth replied, "We doubt it."

Now, in Luke 5, Jesus was in another place teaching doctors of the Law — men who had memorized the whole Old Testament. They had doubts about Him, too.

Never be discouraged when you've got a room full of sad-looking, unbelieving faces, because someone is on the way to the roof! Someone is always on the way to their miracle.

Just keep saying, "This is it, now is the time, this is the day, and the anointing of the Holy Spirit is here. Someone is going to believe God. Someone is on the way to the roof right now!"

Knocking a Hole From the Natural to the Supernatural

Never underestimate the power of an act of faith for you, your family, and your future. I believe that acts of faith are being recorded in what I call *God's Book of Exploits.*

This book of remembrance is still being written about you, your family, your city, and your nation. Every time you do something in faith, God says, "Write that down. Get that in the library!" Never underestimate the power of believing God and declaring what He says.

The Lord once showed me a vision of people running, jumping, dancing, and laughing. He showed me people jumping through a hole into the power of God and getting the manifestation of their miracle!

I asked, "What is that, Lord?"

He said, "That's Luke 5. People have been jumping through the hole those five men knocked from the natural to the supernatural and receiving their miracle for the last 2,000 years."

People have been reading that Bible story and saying, "I believe I can get my miracle. I believe I can knock a hole in the roof and jump through."

That hole is big enough for you, your family, your friends, and your city. It's even big enough for a whole nation.

If people do not understand the fight of faith, they also will not understand the peace and the tranquility that fills your heart once you've knocked your hole in the roof and sat at the feet of Jesus.

Whatever it takes, get to the feet of Jesus! Once you get there, everything will be all right.

Real Bible Faith

Often we want some *easy* faith. Do you think the devil is going to let you say faith confessions without coming around and attacking you?

You get angry when you see other people get their miracle. You said a few things on the way to the house, but you wouldn't go up on the roof, because you were too embarrassed and didn't want to face the pain. Go ahead — go onto the roof and let them knock a hole in it for you.

Real Bible faith doesn't get embarrassed. It is not timid, and it is not self-conscious or conscious of people. Real Bible faith says, "This is it — Jesus and me — now! I'm not doing this to impress anyone. I'm not trying to show anyone how spiritual I am. I need something from Jesus that I know I can't get any other way."

Jesus Is Looking for Faith

You need to knock a hole in your roof. If you've got a body, you've got authority in the Earth. If you've got a voice, you've got authority in the Earth. Can you move? Good. Jesus can work with you. He's looking for faith.

Jesus was a great faith preacher. While He was teaching, the atmosphere got charged with faith because of the Word of God. Everything you can see was created by the Word of God. Faith is the material that makes up every thing. And faith itself is made up of two major parts — believing and speaking.

When faith starts believing and speaking, it starts acting like what it's believing and speaking. It starts moving in that direction. Your body may shake with fear, but your spirit will move.

When Jesus saw the faith of the sick man and his friends, He recognized that it was corporate faith. There is a fight to faith. The faith walk is not necessarily the easiest road. It's a challenging road, but it's also a glory road. If you believe, you'll see the glory, like the paralyzed man did.

Luke 5:20 records, **"When he [Jesus] saw their faith, he said unto him, Man, thy sins are forgiven thee."**

Jesus was doing faith surgery. The scribes and the Pharisees were shocked, but Jesus knew what they were thinking.

He asked them, starting in verse 22:

...What reason ye in your hearts? Whether is easier, to say, Thy sins be forgiven thee; or to say, Rise up and walk? But that ye may know that the Son of man hath power upon earth to forgive sins, (he said unto the sick of the palsy,) I say unto thee, Arise, and take up thy couch, and go into thine house. And immediately he rose up before them, and took up that whereon he lay, and departed to his own house, glorifying God. And they were all amazed, and they glorified God, and were filled with fear, saying, We have seen strange things to day.

Luke 5:22-26

As Jesus told the doctors of the Law, His ability was not the issue. He had the willingness and the power to forgive sins and to heal the sick. Furthermore, all things are possible to the person who believes.

Living by Faith

Living by faith is different from trying to use your faith every once in a while. Living by faith means getting up in the morning and choosing to walk by faith, not by sight. Then, in the afternoon, when you have an opportunity to declare the way you feel or the way things look, you've got to say what God says.

Smith Wigglesworth said, "God has designed that the just shall live by faith." God *has*.

Kenneth E. Hagin didn't make this up; Wigglesworth didn't make this up; and Oral Roberts didn't make this up. This didn't come out of Tulsa; it came out of Nazareth! God has designed that the just shall live by faith.

I carry *Ever Increasing Faith*, the book about Wigglesworth, with me everywhere I go. Once I've read it through, I start reading it again. I want to find out more about his faith walk. He raised 24 people from the dead, and he was a prosperous man, too. When he went into the ministry, he told the Lord, "I'll always wear the best."

Your faith will work whichever way you turn it, but you've got to get it focused on something, and you've got to have confidence. God is arranging things and putting them within the reach of your faith; however, sometimes there is a stretch of water that has to be walked on before you get your miracle.

The scribes and the Pharisees admitted they had seen "strange things" that day. God wants to do some "strange things" in our day, too. Of course, these things will not seem strange to those of us who know the Bible.

We live by faith, and we walk by faith. We fight the good fight of faith. We hold fast to our confession of faith. We know all things are possible to those who believe.

Jesus is looking for faith. Jesus asked, **"...when the Son of man cometh, shall he find faith on the earth?"** (Luke 18:8). It takes faith to move with God. It takes faith to obey God. It takes faith to please God.

Confess right now: "I have the spirit of faith. I believe and I speak. I have a measure of the God-kind of faith, and that measure is growing. I have over-coming faith — mountain-moving faith."

Jesus said, **"...whosoever shall say unto this mountain, Be thou removed, and be thou cast into the sea; and shall not doubt in his heart, but shall believe that those things which he saith..."** (Mark 11:23).

I have the same kind of faith that created the world in the beginning. I have a measure of the God-kind of faith, and it's framing my world with blessing, healing, victory, and prosperity. I believe and I speak!

The SPIRIT OF FAITH

is necessary

not only

to RECEIVE

GOD'S BEST

BLESSINGS, but

also to FOLLOW

GOD'S PLAN

FOR YOUR LIFE.

9
Growing Faith

In the book *Ever Increasing Faith*, Smith Wigglesworth is quoted as having said many profound things about faith. Two major areas in the book are living by faith and being filled with the Holy Spirit.

As you study the Book of Acts, you'll find the people were full of faith and the Holy Spirit. Those two things are really important. If you are expecting miracles, you must learn how to walk by faith and be filled with the Spirit. God is raising up men and women like this today.

I believe Smith Wigglesworth was an apostle of faith. If you are serious about walking and living by faith, you must study not only the Word of God, but also the lives of men and women God has anointed to be apostles, prophets, evangelists, pastors, and teachers. God has anointed them to speak the Word of God and to write the word of faith to this generation.

The Lord said it to me this way: "You've got to get it before you get it. Once you get it, you'll get it. Once you get it, you'll act like you've got it. Then, once you've got it, you can say, 'I've got it. I'm not trying to get it, I don't hope to get it. I've got it.'"

In Mark 11:24, Jesus said, **"...What things soever ye desire, when ye pray, believe that ye receive them, and ye shall have them."** And in Matthew 13:12, Jesus said, **"For whosoever hath, to him shall be given, and he shall have more abundance: but whosoever hath not, from him shall be taken away even that he hath."**

Once you get faith for it on the inside, you get it on the outside. *Now* faith is. Believe God.

As we saw earlier, Dr. Yeomans commented, "God delights in His children stepping out over the aching void with nothing under their feet but the Word of God."' When I read that statement, the first thing I thought about was someone stepping over a cliff with nothing under his feet but the Word of God.

The second thing I thought about was, "God delights." I wondered, "What makes Him so happy?" I believe that, because He is a faith God, everything is created by faith. I believe we will have to exercise our faith throughout eternity, and things will be created with faith.

I believe God delights over His children, like you delight when your little child crawls and then takes steps. I believe God is just like that. As our daddy, He is saying, "Come on, let Me show you how I walk. Let Me show you how things work. Let Me show you how to receive. Let Me show you how to be blessed." When you start to take little steps, I believe He smiles and says, "Look at him! Look at that!"

The devil will do everything he can to get you in the sense realm or the feeling realm. When this happens, simply say, "I'm not going."

Brother Hagin has said, "If the devil can get you out of the arena of faith, he'll whip you. If he can get you into the arena of sight and feelings and circumstances, he'll whip you every time."

Make the devil come into the arena of faith; that is where you always win!

Cleared for 40,000 Feet

I like the way one preacher described growing faith. As he was taking off in his jet one day, the control tower said, "You're cleared for 10,000 feet." The plane rose to 10,000 feet. In a little while, the control tower said, "You're cleared for 20,000 feet."

The preacher flew up to 20,000 feet. Then the tower said, "You're cleared for 40,000 feet," so he went up to 40,000 feet. The man in the control tower knows things you don't know. You can't say, "I'm going to fly wherever I want to."

Likewise, Jesus is the Author and the Finisher of your faith. Faith is obeying God. You must wait until you've got clearance to climb to higher spiritual altitudes.

My preacher friend said that while he was climbing higher, the Lord spoke to him, saying, "I wish you had as much confidence in Me as you do in that man in the control tower. When I tell you that you are cleared for 20,000 feet, pull the throttle back and head for it."

You know when you are cleared in your spirit. When you have the spirit of faith, you know how your faith works. You've already exercised your faith, and you know if something is troubling you, you'd better stay at 20,000 feet until something on the inside of you — the Holy Spirit — says that you are cleared for 40,000 feet. When He says you are, just pull the throttle back. That's the way your faith grows.

10

Faith Challenges

Most people do not understand the challenge or the fight of faith. It's easy to talk faith and learn all the words until you face some challenges in your life — until you learn to walk by faith and not by sight.

"Few people understand except those who have battled the fierce ways and the darkness of the night, and the difficulty," one faith pioneer noted.

Jesus told the Syrophoenician woman who came to Him pleading for her daughter's healing, **"Let the children first be filled..."** (Mark 7:27-29).

Jesus wanted to heal her daughter, but He recognized she didn't have the faith to receive it. So He just stopped and kept working on her to see if her faith could come up a notch. When it did, He said, "It's done. Your daughter is healed!"Dr. Yeomans said He was really doing surgery on her faith!

Some people claim, "I'm trying God." But God can't be tried; He is already proven. Sometimes your faith may be tested by God or circumstances. God can always take the simplest thing, help you receive it, and take you up another notch in your faith.

Your Faith Works Anytime

Your walk of faith may run through stormy waters. When Peter walked on the water (Matthew 14:25-33), it seemed as if the Lord picked the worst time. It was 3 o'clock in the morning, the waves were high, and the winds were blowing when Jesus came walking toward the disciples over the water.

Peter asked, "Lord, is that You? I want to come to You." Jesus said, "Come"— one word. He didn't say, "Come on, you can do it!" People criticize Peter for sinking, but they forget he's the only one who got out of the boat!

It seems as if God always picks the time when it looks like you're the weakest and you can't do it. Peter could have said, "Lord, could we try this tomorrow afternoon?" People always have suggestions for God. What He wants to do doesn't fit into their schedule at the time. But God picks that time to show that faith in Him will work anytime, anywhere, and for anyone who will believe Him.

Announce the Outcome in the Middle of the Battle

I like the apostle Paul's attitude in the middle of a storm. In Acts 27:25, he said, "Wherefore, sirs, be of good cheer: for I believe God, that it shall be even as it was told me."

He didn't say he wasn't having a storm; he simply said, "I'm going over; I'm not going under. There might be a storm, but I believe God, and everything's going to be all right."

That takes a spirit of faith. After they arrive safely on the shore, some people like to brag about how much they believed during the storm. "I tell you, I knew everything was going to be all right, Pastor." Where were they when all the others on board were hanging over the side of the boat, throwing up and moaning, "We're all going to die in this storm!"

The spirit of faith will announce the outcome in the middle of the battle, in the middle of the trial, in the middle of the struggle, in the middle of the challenge.

The spirit of faith will say, "I'm getting happy right now, because I have a word from God. God said, 'Everything is going to be all right.' I believe God. It shall be even as He told me."

Performance of Your Faith

Dr. Yeomans, a medical doctor, wrote that when she was dying of drug addiction, another woman, who was dying of cancer, was with her.

When I was addicted to morphine and at my last gasp, I had a lovely friend, a beautiful woman, cultured, wealthy, and, most important, deeply spiritual. She lived in her Bible and lived it out in her daily life...

She and I had a strange experience that drew us very close together. We were dying at the same time, she of a malignant growth, I of morphine addiction, hopeless cases both of them.

We used to sit together "beside the silent sea," waiting the sound of "the muffled oar" with our Bibles open in front of us. As we turned the leaves we found them "leaves of healing," for there was divine healing on every page. But we could not seem to grasp it, for there was a stretch of water to be walked upon.

How to take the leap? Yet it must be done if we were to survive. We were not afraid to go, and yet we felt as though we ought to be healed in view of God's promises.

At last I somehow got out of the boat and walked on the water. I think God had to make it nearly capsize to get me out. When I saw the waves boisterous and I sank, He caught me. By this time my lovely friend had been taken by her devoted husband to some sanitarium where, though I tried my best, I could not reach her. I never saw her again...

Then I heard that Voice. He said, "Walk on the water. You have been looking for improvements in symptoms, a change in the natural order of things. Stop it. That isn't it at all. My word is absolutely true. My healing is supernatural. It doesn't matter how you feel. *Step out.*" And I did.[1]

Faith says, "I believe I have it." The "performance department" is God's department. In other words, your department is to walk on the Word, keep your eyes and expectation on Jesus, and keep moving.

Wigglesworth said it this way: "There have been times when I have been pressed through circumstances and it seemed as if a dozen railroad engines were going over me, but I have found that the hardest things are just lifting places into the grace of God.

We have such a lovely Jesus. He always proves himself to be such a mighty deliverer. He never fails to plan the best things for us."

I'm so glad Wigglesworth said that, because years later people can read it when they are crying out in the midst of difficulties and challenges.

Cry Out for Jesus

When you hang out around faith people, you'll hear cries every now and then of, "Jesus, help me!" The ministry of Jesus was like that. People were hollering to Him all the time.

The Syrophoenician woman hollered (Matthew 15:22). Blind Bartimaeus cried out for mercy (Mark 10:48). Peter said, "Lord, save me!" (Matthew 14:30). The only people who hollered were people who believed God but needed to make an adjustment in their faith.

When you start sinking, ask, "What am I supposed to do?" You can sink, you can change your philosophy, you can do whatever you want to do, or you can cry and say, "Lord, what am I doing wrong?"

Some people would rather sink than ask the Lord what they're doing wrong. I'd rather ask Him, "What am I doing wrong?"

The other disciples were scared when they saw Peter get out of the boat and walk on the water. Sometimes a stretch of water must be walked on before you can get to Jesus for the miracle you need.

Swing Out Over Hell and Spit in the Devil's Eye

Some people think they can bypass walking by faith. They think, "That's really good for those faith people — if you're in that camp." But there is only one camp — God the Father of glory and the Father of our Lord Jesus Christ. He is a faith God. Whatever denomination you are, you might as well learn this: The just shall live by faith!

Jesus is looking for faith. Use your faith to go from riding a bicycle to owning a really nice car. Then you can say, "Look what the Lord provided for me as I used my faith." Don't be embarrassed about that. The Bible says not to despise the day of small beginnings. God wants you to have nice things, because you represent Him. You're an ambassador for the Lord Jesus Christ.

So don't sit back and say, "I wish I didn't have these challenges." It may not look like it or feel like it, but it shall be as He told you. You have the Word on it. You are not moved by feelings or impressions; you are moved by the Word.

Wigglesworth said, "I'm not moved by what I see, I'm not moved by what I feel, I'm moved only by what I believe, and I believe God."

The spirit of faith makes you swing out over hell on a corn stalk and spit in the devil's eye.

When
your FAITH
is in ACTION,
it SHOWS UP on
God's radar screen
and HE RELEASES
HIS POWER
to you.

11
Faith Can Be Seen

God not only demands faith of us; He has provided the means whereby we can get faith: **"So then faith cometh by hearing, and hearing by the word of God"** (Romans 10:17). God's Word is "faith food."

Faith "cometh"! And when faith "cometh," fear "goeth," and the devil "runneth." Faith brings God's power on the scene.

God is looking for faith. We know that faith pleases Him. Second Chronicles 16:9 says, **"For the eyes of the Lord run to and fro throughout the whole earth, to shew himself strong in the behalf of them whose heart is perfect toward him...."**

One way you can act on your faith is to start saying and believing the same thing God says. Believe and speak. Say whatever God says. Another way you can act on the Word of God is to start releasing your faith. Act like it's true!

Wigglesworth said, "I'm not moved by what I see. I'm not moved by what I feel. I'm moved by what I believe, and I believe God." Faith will move you.

Four Crazy Friends

In Luke 5:20, when the paralyzed man was healed, Jesus saw the faith of his friends. At that time, Jesus was teaching an educated crowd — Pharisees and doctors of the Law. The Bible says the power of God was present to heal, but none of them got healed.

At the end of Luke 5, the Bible says these educated men went away amazed. When you believe God and receive your victory, even your critics will admit, "Something is going on in his life."

Dr. Yeomans explained in her book *The Great Physician* that a cluster of diamonds has a brilliance that a solitaire never has. In other words, diamonds are most effectively displayed on a black background. The darker the background, the more brilliant the diamonds.[1]

In His encounter with the doctors of the Law, Jesus was teaching in the midst of the darkest, most determined unbelief — and it was not an individual's unbelief; it was national, corporate unbelief!

These doctors of the Law had come from every city and village throughout the whole region to criticize Jesus. However, in the middle of their most persistent, educated unbelief, five flashing "faith diamonds" came through the roof!

Everyone needs at least four crazy friends who will believe that God can do anything — and now is the time for Him to do it!

"When Jesus saw their faith...." The Bible doesn't say He was looking for their luxury car. It doesn't say He saw how nicely they were dressed. It doesn't say He saw their stylish hairdos or how much education they had. He was looking for *faith*.

When some people get blessed, they think they can quit living by faith. No, the just shall live by faith. Even after you get your nice car, your jet, and your big house, and after all your family is saved, you still must live by faith. Living by faith is not something you do every once in a while; it's a daily walk with God.

Faith Comes by Hearing and Hearing

In Acts 14, the apostle Paul perceived that a crippled man had faith to be healed.

And there they preached the gospel. And there sat a certain man at Lystra impotent in his feet, being cripple from his mother's womb, who never had walked. The same heard Paul speak: who stedfastly beholding him, and perceiving that he had faith to be healed, Said with a loud voice, Stand upright on thy feet. And he leaped and walked.

Acts 14:7-10

Faith comes by hearing, and hearing by the Word of God. While Paul was preaching the Gospel, the man had faith to be healed. Paul was preaching Luke 4:18, 19: Jesus not only died for our sins, but He took our

85

sicknesses and diseases, and He also took our poverty, shame, guilt, and depression.

This was the same anointing Jesus had, except now Jesus had died and been raised from the dead and His power has been released toward believers.

Paul saw that the crippled man had faith to be healed, and it kept him in the realm of faith. Before the man could think about it, Paul said, "Stand up on your feet!" The crippled man shouted, leaped — and walked!

Release Your Faith

James 2:17 says, **"Release your faith; act on your faith!"** That man could have started thinking, "If I could stand up on my feet, I wouldn't be sitting here right now." *Reasoning and unbelief will keep you out of God's best blessings.*

Some people disguise unbelief as wisdom. They say, "The intelligent thing to do is..." Your intelligence will see no mighty work.

Some people are afraid to "lose their minds"— to let go of their own thinking, opinions, and traditions. They are afraid to let go and let God have His way.

"Lose your mind" and get the mind of Christ — the mind of the Anointed One and His anointing.

God's Radar Screen

I believe that God has a radar screen in heaven that only shows faith working. He is like an air traffic controller. He can see incoming faith — the location and the movement of faith. When your faith is in action, it shows up on God's radar screen, and He releases His power to you.

Whenever someone gets in faith, God says, "Faith cometh!" Whenever He finds faith, He can do miracles. Mountains will be removed. Sickness will leave. Demons will flee. Creative power will be released.

When patience is mixed with your faith, it keeps you on target and keeps you in the air until you get to the landing strip where you receive.

Do you want to be on God's giant radar screen? He's looking for people to get in faith by believing the Word, speaking the Word, walking by faith, praising Him, thanking Him for His Word, and holding fast to their confession of faith. When you do that, you will show up on that radar screen, and the Father will say, "Faith incoming!"

Faith has to *land* before it gets the miracle. As we saw in Romans 10:17, "So then faith cometh by hearing, and hearing by the word of God." I always say this: When faith cometh, you knoweth. When faith cometh, something happens in your inner man.

Psalm 18:28 says, **"The Lord will light my candle."** When He lights your candle, you can run through a troop and leap over a wall (verse 29). There is no problem outside of you that one light — the fire of the Word of God in your inner man — cannot handle. You can run through that troop, jump over that wall, and move that mountain!

At times, people appear on God's "faith" radar screen, do well, and come in for a landing — the manifestation of God's promise. But all of a sudden something happens, and they go off the screen!

Doubt or fear came in, and the devil said, "How do you feel? How do things look? Do you think you're ever going to be different? Do you think things will ever change for you? Do you think you'll ever do what God has called you to do? Do you think you'll ever get your healing?"

When this happens, you get out of the Spirit and into your thinking and reasoning and into your sight. You go off the screen, and God the Father says, "Oh my, we've got a crash here somewhere. He went off the screen. Someone go and find him!" Someone finds him and gets him back into believing God and speaking the Word. Then he comes back on the screen.

Some people stay on the screen for several days at a time, but they go off the screen as soon as the devil attacks them. God wants you to stay on the screen.

Every morning as soon as you get up, you ought to show up on that radar screen speaking the word of faith: "The Lord is my shepherd; I shall not want. The Lord is my light and my salvation; whom shall I fear? The Lord is the strength of my life." You are back on the screen!

Jesus is always looking for faith. You may wonder, "What is faith?" The palsied man's friends spoke words of faith: "This is it. Now is the time. We believe. This is the day. All we've got to do is get in the presence of Jesus."

Jesus saw their faith. He is still looking for faith today, but not yesterday's faith. He is asking, "What do you believe today? What are you declaring today? What are you acting on today?"

EVERYONE NEEDS
at least
FOUR "CRAZY"
FRIENDS who
believe
that with God
ALL THINGS ARE
POSSIBLE!

12
Corporate Faith

In Luke 5, when the palsied man's friends lowered him through the roof, Jesus saw corporate faith in action. That's the power of believers pulling together. If you can get several believers pulling together in any church, faith will be much stronger than unbelief.

Faith is what Jesus was looking for. I believe He said, "I only need 12 believers." Once He got the 12 disciples, He went for 70 more. God is always on the increase. When Jesus had the 70, He believed for 120 believers to come together, and they did, in the Upper Room.

Smith Wigglesworth said that it is always a trap of the devil to try to make you independent. We need one another, and we need to submit to one another. This is corporate faith.

The apostle Paul was glad that a few disciples were holding the ropes of the basket when he was being lowered over the Damascus town wall, escaping persecution (Acts 9:25). Later, he was more important than they were, but at that moment, they were more important than he was!

While holding the ropes, they probably thought they'd like to do something significant for the Lord someday, but perhaps helping Paul escape was the most significant thing they ever did. They were holding in a basket the man who went on to write more than half the New Testament.

We need one another, but if the devil can trick you into being independent, he can get you out of a place of faith. Corporate faith is the way God has chosen for us to help one another. We dare not be independent.

God wants to bring us to a place where we submit ourselves to one another. If we refuse, we will get away from the Word of God and out of the place of faith.

Faith Friends

Wigglesworth said, "I went to a meeting one time and I was very, very sick and got worse. I knew the perfect will of God was for me to humble myself and ask the elders to pray for me. I put it off and the meeting finished. I went home without being anointed and prayed with. Everyone in the house caught the illness I had."

We dare not be independent. Never get so proud of your faith that you think that you don't need any faith help. When your faith wavers, you have faith friends who will encourage you. I thank God for faith friends! Most of us are alive because of faith friends —

people who kept believing God and kept believing in us when we didn't even believe in ourselves.

God has planned great things for you, and they're just ahead. The devil is trying to get you to stop one step before your miracle.

The just shall live by faith. I have a spirit of faith. I hang around people with a spirit of faith. I hang around people who have more faith than I do. I'm flying at 20,000 feet, but their faith has grown to where they're flying at 40,000 feet. I'm going to hang around them and find out how they pulled back and made it to 40,000 feet. After all, God is no respecter of persons.

The people I hang around with have wet sandals. That means they got out of the boat. That means when they began to sink, Jesus pulled them up.

The Church of the Lord Jesus Christ — the Body of Christ — with all its imperfections is still the best place in the whole world to be. You might find a lot of things wrong with the Church, but it's still the best place to be. Don't allow the devil to make you independent.

Make this confession: "I've got faith friends, and I'm hanging out with them. They're not perfect friends, but God is working on them just like He's working on me."

FAITH MOVES GOD.

FAITH moves mountains.

FAITH won't move anything

until it moves you.

———————

The first part of you that

your FAITH will move is

your mouth.

GOD IS A FAITH GOD.

13

Jubilee Faith

Jesus began his earthly ministry when He gave His first message in the synagogue at Nazareth. He said:

The Spirit of the Lord is upon me, because he hath anointed me to preach the gospel to the poor; he hath sent me to heal the broken-hearted, to preach deliverance to the captives, and recovering of sight to the blind, to set at liberty them that are bruised, To preach the acceptable year of the Lord. And he closed the book, and he gave it again to the minister, and sat down. And the eyes of all them that were in the synagogue were fastened on him. And he began to say unto them, This day is this scripture fulfilled in your ears.

Luke 4:18-21

Jesus was reading from Isaiah 61. He said, "Isaiah said this...Isaiah was talking about Me. I'm the person. I'm the Messiah, the Anointed One. Now is the time, and this is it. Today I'm preaching the acceptable year of the Lord." *The Amplified Bible* translates this, "The year when salvation and the free favors of God will profusely abound."[1]

Jesus was really talking about the Year of Jubilee, when the Messiah would come and announce, "This is the Year of Jubilee!" Leviticus 25 explains in detail all the events that happened in a Year of Jubilee.

Every fiftieth year, God declared a Year of Jubilee — a year of celebration — in the nation of Israel. Jubilee was the year when debts were canceled. Anything you had lost — houses, lands, furniture, anything — had to come back to you. It was the year of righteousness. It was also the year of supernatural increase. God said, "What you plant this year will be so blessed, you'll have an increase that will last for three years."

Jubilee Is Supernatural

Jubilee was an unusual time. Every fiftieth year God said, "It's a Year of Jubilee, and I'm changing the whole economy." This means, God can actually afford to tell the economy to do whatever He wants it to do.

God said, "In this fiftieth year, if you've been bound, you go free. If you're in debt, you go free. If you've lost your land, it's got to come back to you. It's a time of Jubilee, a time of celebration, a happy time."

Jesus added financial prosperity to Jubilee. Jubilee is supernatural debt cancellation, supernatural blessing, and supernatural increase that cannot be fully explained in the natural.

In the gospels, we see Jesus operating in signs and wonders when it came to material things. Signs and wonders made it possible for Him to use five loaves and two fishes to feed 5,000 people. Signs and wonders made it possible for Him to catch a fish and pay His taxes with the coin that was in its mouth.

The supernatural is the added ingredient in Jubilee. Jesus gave the first ingredient when He announced, "Now is the time!" The second ingredient is the anointing of the Holy Spirit. The Spirit of God will come upon you to perform it. The third ingredient is the message you see in the Gospel. However, you must mix faith with the Word of God to have your Jubilee.

Freedom From Sickness and Poverty

After Jesus announced the beginning of Jubilee and financial prosperity, He added freedom from sickness.

Acts 10:38 tells us, **"How God anointed Jesus of Nazareth with the Holy Ghost and with power who went about doing good, and healing all that were oppressed of the devil; for God was with him."**

Sickness is satanic oppression; it is not from God. God anointed Jesus with the Holy Ghost and power, and He went about doing good and healing *all*. Is it God's will to heal all? Yes, because Jesus went about doing good and healing *all*.

We can see the same thing in Matthew 8:16, where, again, Jesus healed all who were sick: **"When the even was come, they brought unto him many that were possessed with devils: and he cast out the spirits with his word, and he healed all that were sick."**

This means there is no case too hard for Him to heal. The devil can't come up with a case that is too difficult for Jesus. From the top of your head to the soles of your feet, Jesus is a Specialist in all areas of internal and external medicine. He has the cure for your body and your life. He is the cure!

God anointed Him with the Holy Spirit and power. If He was pronouncing a Year of Jubilee, it would seem like everyone in Nazareth would have understood and accepted it, and everyone in the vicinity of Jesus would have received miracles.

However, we can see from reading Luke 4 that every one in Nazareth *didn't* get it, and they didn't receive miracles. They didn't receive the supernatural — supernatural debt cancellation, supernatural healing, and freedom from oppression.

The Anointing Follows Faith

In His sermon in Nazareth, Jesus spoke of the brokenhearted. He was referring to people who have been broken by life, disappointed and hurt, and their lives left in chaos.

Did you know the anointing is smart? It will go right to the point of your need. Once you learn how to use your faith, *the anointing will follow the line of faith.* The Jubilee anointing — Jesus' anointing — always follows the line of faith.

Jesus' anointing or Jubilee comes where there is faith. People can be in the vicinity of Jubilee anointing and never receive anything. They can be in the vicinity of the power of God in operation and never receive anything. You must exercise faith to receive because God is a faith God.

As Wigglesworth said, "It seems like God will pass over a million people just to find somebody who believes Him." Wouldn't you be disappointed if God passed over you and blessed someone next to you? That would really be sad. God is always trying to find someone who will believe Him.

Remember, Jesus asked, "...when the Son of man cometh, shall he find faith on the earth?" Why did He say that? Because faith is the first thing He looks for.

EVERY
BREAKTHROUGH
in FAITH
comes from a
BREAKTHROUGH
in REVELATION
KNOWLEDGE.

14

Faith Releases Power

The apostle Paul prayed powerful prayers that were full of faith. One of the best known of these prayers is found in the first chapter of Ephesians.

That the God of our Lord Jesus Christ, the Father of glory, may give unto you the spirit of wisdom and revelation in the knowledge of him: The eyes of your understanding being enlightened; that ye may know what is the hope of his calling, and what the riches of the glory of his inheritance in the saints, And what is the exceeding greatness of his power to usward who believe, according to the working of his mighty power, Which he wrought in Christ, when he raised him from the dead, and set him at his own right hand in the heavenly places.

Ephesians 1:17-20

Did you notice what Paul said about the "exceeding greatness" of God's power? It is released to us who believe, according to the working of His mighty power that He wrought in Christ when He raised Him from the dead. In other words, the power of God is released toward believers. Doubters get nothing!

God's power is "exceeding" great power. People who have heard about it and know the Gospel will say, "I know Jesus has power; I know the Gospel is the power of God; I know God is a mighty God." But they don't know that it only works toward believers. The power of God follows a line of faith.

Paul said, "It's the same power that raised Christ from the dead." Whatever that power did when it raised Christ from the dead, it will do the same thing in your spirit, your soul, and your body. It will do everything in your body except give you an immortal or glorified body, because you will get that at the Rapture.

God has released enough power to heal you and to drive sickness out of your body. Exceeding great power — unlimited power — is released toward the believer!

Check Your "Believer"

The power of God could be present, but if you are not a believer, or if you don't have your "switch of faith" turned on, you won't get a thing. People do have such a "switch," but they often do not know where it is or how to turn it on.

The power of God is released toward believers. If you have been saying, "I don't ever feel any power; I don't see any mountains moving; I don't see anything changing in my life," you'd better check your "believer" and see how it is doing.

If you are born again, the Bible calls you a believer. Whoever heard of an unbelieving believer? If you are a believer, go ahead and believe.

That's what I do: I believe. I'm a believer, so I believe God. I believe the Bible. I believe Jesus is alive. I believe the same power that raised Him from the dead is working right now.

Someone said it this way: "Religion worships God for what He did while it fights what He's doing." In other words, religion always wants to discuss the God of the past — the God of the Old Testament or the God of the days of Jesus.

Religious people say, "If only I had been there when Jesus walked the shore of the Sea of Galilee. If only I had been there to see those miracles!"

But these religious people would probably have been listed in Luke 5 as those who sat there and didn't do any thing. They would have been those who were well versed in the scriptures but looked at Jesus and said, "I don't know...He might not be it, and this might not be the day. The power might not be present. I might get it, but I might not get it."

They would have been sitting there as spectators, like the Pharisees and the doctors of the Law, full of head knowledge, not realizing that Jesus — the power of God — was standing right in front of them!

See the Glory of God

Messiah was standing right in front of them! Jubilee was standing right in front of them! *Healing* was standing right in front of them! *Deliverance* was standing right in front of them! Everything the Old Testament had prophesied about the Messiah was standing right in front of them that day!

Jesus said, "They missed the day of their visitation." God was doing something significant, and they — the doctors of the Law — totally missed it!

Jesus said in John 11:40, **"If you believe, you will see the glory of God."** If you don't see any glory, you'd better check your "believer," because if you do believe, you will see the glory.

The glory is the manifested presence of God. It is present not simply to give you goosebumps but to change things in your life, move mountains, heal your body, cancel your debts, bless you abundantly, bring Jubilee to you, and make you happy.

Faith Pleases God

Some people say, "I don't think all that faith business is important." Hebrews 11:6 says, **"Without faith it is impossible to please him: for he that cometh** to God must believe that he is, and that he is a rewarder of them that diligently seek him."

Without faith it is impossible to please God! God is a faith God. You will be frustrated with Him if you don't understand that He is a faith God, and He is looking for faith. God was a faith God in the Old Testament. Jesus in the New Testament is "God with us," and He is looking for faith.

Jesus told the woman with the issue of blood, **"...Daughter, *thy faith* hath made thee whole..."** (Mark 5:34). Notice He didn't say, "Daughter, my great power, my anointing, and the Jubilee has made you whole."

No, He said, "...Daughter, thy faith hath made thee whole...." It was this woman's faith that activated the Jubilee, the anointing, and the power.

The
SPIRIT
OF FAITH
knocks a hole
from the natural
to the
SUPERNATURAL.

15
Mighty Miracles Require Faith

We know God is able to do all things. Nothing is impossible with God! We know that God cannot lie. People say, "It's up to God. If God wants to do it, God can do anything. He's a sovereign God."

Apparently, Jesus didn't know that. If God can do anything anytime He wants to, why didn't Jesus do it right there in His own hometown?

Mark 6:5, 6 says, **"And he could there do no mighty work, save that he laid his hands upon a few sick folk, and healed them. And he marvelled because of their unbelief. And he went round about the villages, teaching."**

Can you imagine Jesus being frustrated because He wanted to do a mighty work, but He couldn't? The original Greek implies that He tried, but He couldn't.

What is a *mighty* work? It is a demonstration of His power and His glory. Jesus wanted to do something great — a mighty work — but He couldn't. He did lay hands on a few sickly people. Other translations call them, "A few people with minor ailments."

I believe Jesus wanted to do some mighty Jubilee miracles — some mighty demonstrations of His power — but because of unbelief, He couldn't do any mighty work. I wonder what He would say about us today?

Two Kinds of Unbelief

Verse 6 says, "And he marvelled because of their unbelief...." Jesus said, "I've never seen such unbelief," but He knew that the cure for their unbelief was for Him to go to their cities and villages and teach.

There are two kinds of unbelief. The first is simply *ignorance of the Word*. People don't know that it's the year of Jubilee, that Jesus is anointed, or what faith is. They don't know that faith requires action, and believing requires a confession.

The cure for that kind of unbelief is teaching, so Jesus went to all the surrounding cities and the villages, teaching.

He said, in effect, "The Spirit of the Lord is upon Me. He has anointed Me. This is the year of Jubilee. It is time for you to go free. Healing does belong to you. You can be healed of brokenheartedness. You can get out of debt. You can be blessed coming in and going out. This is the time of blessing. This is it! You can get the anointing from Me, but you need to get it right now. Today the scripture is fulfilled in your ears!"

Jesus went about trying to cure the first kind of unbelief, ignorance of the Word. As we have seen, the cure is found in Romans 10:17, **"Faith cometh by hearing, and hearing by the word of God."**

How does faith come? Where does faith come from? Whatever you need faith for, the Bible has the answer. Someone said it this way: "The whole Bible is not about faith, but the whole Bible does have the capacity to produce faith for whatever you need to receive from God."

Whether it's salvation, the baptism in the Holy Spirit, divine healing, financial blessing, your marriage, your family, or whatever else you may need help with — the answer is already written in the Word.

The faith of someone who believes will cause a beam of light to pierce through unbelief all the way up to heaven, and the anointing will follow that line of faith back to Earth and release the power of God!

Educated Unbelief

The second kind of unbelief is what the Pharisees and the doctors of the Law showed in Luke 5 — unpersuadableness to act on the Word of God or educated unbelief.

When I talk with people like this, they already know the counsel I'm going to give them and can quote scriptures and references. When I give them a scripture, they'll say, "I know that, Pastor, but you don't understand my problem."

No matter how long I counsel them, I can't help them. Although they have been in church and Sunday School for years, they have not been persuaded to act like the Bible is true.

Faith is simply an act. Faith is acting on the Word of God. Faith says, "I believe the Word, and now I'm acting on it. I'm saying what it says. I'm acting like the Bible is true." That's all faith is — being persuaded to act on the Word of God.

James 2:17 says that faith without works is dead. Faith without corresponding action is dead. Because it has no life, it won't change anything in your life.

Some people do have a form of faith, but it's dead faith. Dead faith you have to carry; living faith will carry you. So some have all kinds of props trying to support their faith, but living faith props you up instead of your trying to prop it up.

Small Problem, Big God

When the problems of life come, find out what the Word says, quote it, and act on it. The more you speak the problem, the bigger it will get. But the more you hear the Word, the bigger God gets. He gets bigger and bigger, and your problem gets smaller and smaller.

We serve a mighty God who has exceeding great power. That great power is directed toward us who believe. You need to say, "I'm a believer, not a doubter."

Wouldn't you like to come through a hole in the roof and fall on the head of a Pharisee, who represents a lot of educated unbelief? Jesus would love to see it. As Dr. Yeomans commented, "This unlearned, ignorant man almost fell on the reverent heads of the Pharisees."[1]

Maybe you won't come through a hole in the roof, but you can dance and suddenly stomp on the foot of the Pharisee next to you. Or you can go to church and fall over someone who is trying to figure God out.

You can't figure God out. All you can know is that He's a faith God. You don't have to figure out anything about Him. Nothing is impossible with Him. All things are possible to the person who believes. That's all you need to know about God.

In Luke 5:20, one phrase — "when he saw their faith" — should be underlined in your Bible. It refers to the four friends who brought the palsied man to Jesus for healing. Jesus saw their faith.

All five of them agreed to believe the same thing: Jesus was alive, His anointing and power were present, and that it was the day for healing.

Real Bible faith cannot and will not be denied. Bible faith works! This is where mighty works are to be found.

FAITH
is an act.

The simplest
definition of **FAITH**:
ACTING LIKE THE
BIBLE IS TRUE.

16

Faith Is an Act

Faith is an act. That's the way the Lord explained it to me.

Because I'm rather simple sometimes, I pray and pray, "Lord, I just don't understand this, because your thoughts are higher than our thoughts. I don't quite grasp how to get along with You or how to receive from You. I'm not receiving. My 'receiver' is not working right."

Often we think that everyone ought to know how to receive from God. But if that's true, why did Jesus spend three and a half years teaching people? People didn't pick it up automatically. Jesus had to teach them how to receive from God. He was always teaching, preaching, and healing.

I appreciate the teaching ministry of the Lord Jesus Christ, because He would say it until you got it, even if you flunked out of the third grade and never made it back. Jesus will stick with you until you get it; that is, if you want the help, the blessing, and the miracle.

Get It Before You Get It

The way things work in the Spirit is that you always get it before you get it. Some people never got it; that's why they never got it. If you're saying, "I don't get it," that's why you don't get it.

Jesus said in Mark 11:24, **"...What things soever ye desire, when ye pray, believe that ye receive them, and ye shall have them."** Another translation says, "Believe you've got it, and you'll get it."

You may be thinking, "But I don't have it." That's right. Jesus said, "*Believe* you've received it, and you'll get it." When the devil says, "You don't have it," reply, "That's obvious, but I believe I have received it." You get it on the *inside* — in your spirit — before you ever get it on the *outside*.

The Spirit of Faith Is Contagious

The spirit of faith must be imparted, and the principles of faith must be taught. You need both. The spirit of faith must be caught or imparted from someone who has it. It's contagious.

The apostle Paul said, **"We having the same spirit of faith, according as it is written, I believed, and therefore have I spoken; we also believe, and therefore speak"** (2 Corinthians 4:13). He said, "We have it!" I'm glad he didn't say, "I have it." He was addressing the whole church of Corinth. He was saying, "You've got it, I've got it, and you got it from me."

I love to hang around people who have a spirit of faith — people who believe bigger than I can. That doesn't intimidate or threaten me; it challenges me. God is no respecter of persons; He has no favorites.

If Jesus said you were to have faith, it must not be arrogant to say you've got it. When you walk in faith, some people say, "That's a bit arrogant." But really, if you were hanging around Paul, would you have thought he was arrogant? Would you have thought that Joshua and Caleb were arrogant? When David killed Goliath, would you have thought he was arrogant? When David said that he would pay for the Temple himself with an offering of about $1.4 billion, would you have thought he was arrogant?

In Second Corinthians 4:13, Paul was quoting David when he said, **"I believed and I spoke."** Those are the ingredients of the spirit of faith. David said, "I have the spirit of faith," and obviously he did.

When he was 17 years old, David ran at a giant while everyone else was running away from the giant. To do that, you've got something no one else has. Where did David get that spirit of faith? "Faith cometh by hearing, and hearing by the word of God."

Because David had a spirit of faith, 400 men — David's mighty men — were attracted to join forces with him. However, they weren't mighty when they met David. When they went to the cave of Adullam, they were distressed, discontented, and in debt (1 Samuel 22:2). Those three problems usually hang out together!

Faith and Finances

David spent much time meditating upon the Word of God and receiving revelation (Psalm 1). He was not simply learning words; he was getting to know the Author who spoke the words.

Many people know Bible verses, but the spirit of faith comes from the words that get implanted into you. When you get the Word on the inside of you, you get the spirit of faith that comes straight from God.

Those 400 men caught the spirit of faith from David, and they became David's mighty men (2 Samuel 23:8-23). I believe he taught them about the covenant and about praising and worshipping God. In the Bible you can read about the tremendous things the mighty men did for God and the people of God.

When David brought his offering of $1.4 billion, his mighty men brought their offering of $2.6 billion (1 Chronicles 29:1-9). This dollar amount is the estimated value of the gold and the silver that was given to build the Temple in Jerusalem.

The Spirit of Faith Affects Every Area

The spirit of faith will invade every area of your life. You can't keep God in one little compartment. The spirit of faith actually affects every area of your life, including your physical health, finances, future, business, and relationships.

As we have seen, the spirit of faith comes not only from feeding on the Word of God, but also from hanging around people who have the spirit of faith. David's mighty men got it, and it affected their finances. Instead of being in debt, they gave an offering of an estimated $2.6 billion!

When it comes to faith for finances, some people are stronger than others. There are things that are more important than money, but if you're broke, it's hard to think of them. Psalm 24:1 says, **"The earth is the Lord's, and the fulness thereof...."**

God wants you to have things because He still retains ownership of the Earth, and He wants to bless you for covenant reasons, not for covetous reasons. He gives you power to get wealth to establish His covenant (Deuteronomy 8:18). This is not simply about money; however, the spirit of faith affects the financial area of your life.

You ought to be able to get up every morning saying, "I have the God-kind of faith. I have the same kind of faith that created the worlds in the beginning. I don't have the same measure, but I've got the same kind, and the measure of my faith is increasing."

Wigglesworth said it this way: "Any man may be changed by faith no matter how he may be fettered."

Faith Must Be Used

When you learn how to use the God-kind of faith, whatever has bound you must leave. You become a target for the devil when you have faith, so don't be upset when his attacks come.

You may think, "Since I got hold of all this faith business, it seems like all hell has broken loose." You ought to start laughing, because you know that the devil is trying to get you to renounce your faith. You ought to say, "I'm holding fast to my confession of faith."

If Jesus said you should have the God-kind of faith, it must be possible to have it. And it must be possible to *know* that you have it.

If He told you to have it, there will be times in your life when nothing else will work. You've tried everything — professional help of all kinds — and nothing worked.

But the Holy Spirit is a great Counselor, and the Word of God can get right to the root of the problem. But you must use your faith.

17

Whosoever Shall Have Whatsoever

**For verily I say unto you, That *whosoever*
shall say unto this mountain, Be thou
removed, and be thou cast into the sea; and
shall not doubt in his heart, but shall believe
that those things which he saith shall come
to pass; he shall have *whatsoever* he saith.**

Mark 11:23

Jesus said, "Verily I say unto you...." The word
"verily" means, "I'm telling you the truth." Jesus said
that before He explained exactly how the God-kind of
faith works. Then He said, "Whosoever."

I'm so glad He said, "Whosoever," because I preach
this all over the world. Anyone can do this. It will work
for anyone — whosoever. It will work for the most
stupid person you know. You don't have to be smart to
have faith. If you have been saying, "I'm smart," that's
your biggest problem.

Dr. David Yonggi Cho said that God doesn't talk to
smart people. He only talks to those who say, "Lord,
here I am. Teach me something, Lord."

You can tell someone living in a cardboard box under a bridge about what Jesus did for him, and he will come out from beneath the bridge.

The last word is "whatsoever." Whosoever shall have whatsoever. This will work for anyone and will work on anything. When I found this out, I said, "I'd better start confessing some things. I've just been sitting around trying to watch this thing work. I need to start charting my course."

If faith will work on a mountain, it will work on anything. Sometimes all you need is one word or phrase or one adjustment to make your faith work. It opens you up to the supernatural.

Check What You Have Been Saying

Jesus said, **"Whosoever...shall have whatsoever he saith."** He didn't say, "He can have." He said, "He shall have." To some degree, you do have what you have been saying. If you are not happy with what you have in life, you'd better check out what you have been saying.

When you get serious about this, get a faith partner and say, "Check me out. Watch what I'm saying."

"He shall have those things that he saith." The God kind of faith will work on more than one thing at one time. That means you could confess more than one thing at a time. In your struggling, you have been saying, "I need God to do this or that thing." Realize that God can do many things at the same time, and the lights will not even blink in heaven from an overload! God didn't tell you to get your shovel out and move the mountain; He said, "Speak to it." You don't have to struggle or have a nervous breakdown or heart attack. Speak to your mountain!

Motivate Your Faith

The Bible also says to fight the good fight of faith. I realize that some people don't have any fight in them. Nevertheless, there is a fight to faith. Either you fight the good fight of faith, or you settle for less than God's best. To possess the land, you'll have to fight for it.

You must be motivated to move your mountain, or you'll make friends with it! You'll hoist a white flag and call a truce. The problem is, when you let a mountain stay there very long, it will attract others, and then you'll have a whole mountain range to deal with!

People get personal about their mountains by saying, "My mountain, my situation." This means they've already drawn it on the map of their life, and they plan on its staying there.

One way the Lord motivated me to speak to my mountain was by saying, "If you knew what was on the other side of your mountain, you would move it. You've been letting that thing stay there for years. You don't realize the reason that mountain is there is the devil is trying to keep you from getting something that is just on the other side of that mountain — something I have prepared for you."

In meetings when you get drunk on the Holy Ghost, the Spirit of God will take you up and show you possibilities of what God has ahead for you, and you start laughing. But after the anointing lifts, you're right back to seeing that mountain, and you say, "My God, I thought that thing was gone."

The Holy Ghost lifted you up to show you the possibility, but you'll still have to use your faith to move that mountain. You must say, "I'm talking to you, mountain — right now!"

If you don't know how you got your miracle, you can't get another one, and you could lose the one you've got. Address this mountain, this situation, because God has something good for you. God is not simply good; He's really good. He has said, "I'll do things for you that you wouldn't do for yourself."

You Have To Say Something

Genesis 1 says that the Spirit of God moved on the face of the deep, but nothing happened until God said something. The Holy Spirit will move upon you, but *nothing is going to change until you say something*. You must function with that God-kind of faith.

The God-kind of faith will work for anyone and will work on anything. Jesus said, "You shall have whatsoever you say." Notice, He didn't say that you would have whatsoever is on sale. Some people have a poverty mentality and don't even know it.

This is sad, because it not only limits their receiving, but it also limits their giving. It limits the blessings God wants to give them. God wants to do things through you. Take the limits off, and let God be God.

Jesus didn't say that you would have what others said about you. He said that you have what you say. You say, "When I was growing up, my daddy called me stupid." Jesus didn't say you're going to have what your daddy said; He said you'd have what you said.

Impact the Seen and the Unseen

Jesus said the same thing in Luke 17:5, 6:

And the apostles said unto the Lord, Increase our faith. And the Lord said, If ye had faith as a grain of mustard seed, ye might say unto this sycamine tree, Be thou plucked up by the root, and be thou planted in the sea; and it should obey you.

This was not a "deity trick" that worked in heaven alone. Faith will work for whosoever on whatsoever.

Jesus said it again in Matthew 17:20:

...for verily I say unto you, If ye have faith as

a grain of mustard seed, ye shall say unto this mountain, Remove hence to yonder place; and it shall remove; and nothing shall be impossible unto you.

Here, Jesus is using a mountain in reference to authority over demons and evil spirit. When you speak, your words have an impact not only on the seen but also on the unseen. There are some things I like to say — usually in private — just to make sure they have an impact not only on me but also upon unseen or demonic powers.

When I went to Bible college, I used to say certain things about the blessing of the Lord upon my life and future. Friends would come up to me and say, "You'd better not say that, because the devil will hear you!" I would answer, "I said it for his benefit!" I wanted to make sure he heard me say it.

Run Up the Middle

When I was a little kid, my older brother, Mike, would get his big friends and play football against my little friends and me. I'm almost four years younger than he.

Mike and his team didn't even have a huddle. They would simply walk up to the line and say, "We're going to run straight up the middle and run right over you." They didn't need a huddle for that.

Once you understand your authority as a believer, you'll be able to say, "Devil, I'm going right up the middle, and I'm running right over you!"

Jesus said, "You shall have whatever you *say*." He didn't say you have what you *believe*. The spirit of faith must have both ingredients: believing and speaking.

Your mountain needs to hear your voice. Jesus said, "When you speak to the mountain, it will obey you." By "mountain," He is referring to something that seems too big for you — something that seems impossible for you. But your "mountain" will respond to your voice.

Maintain a Bold Confession

Remember, your individuality is tied up not only in your fingerprints, but also in your voiceprint. Your voice print is a greater definition of your identity than your fingerprint. No other voiceprint is exactly like yours. *Your voice is your address in the Spirit realm.*

When God is about to send something to you, He locates you by your voice. He says, "I recognize that voice!" Then He releases His power, based upon your using your delegated authority.

I like what the Roman centurion said in Matthew 8. Jesus had told him, "I'll come to your house and heal your servant." The centurion replied, "No, you don't need to come to my house. Speak the Word only, and my servant shall be healed" (verse 8).

Jesus was amazed! He turned to His disciples and said, "I have not found such a great faith in all of Israel" (verse 10). It was almost like He was looking for it. I believe that while Jesus was teaching, He was looking around, thinking, "Let Me see if I can find any faith here." He certainly didn't find any faith in his hometown.

Many people want to get to the "whatsoever," because "whatsoever" is available. Whosoever shall have whatsoever. But before you get to the "whatsoever," you must get to the "whosoever." Make a bold, daily confession of who you are "in Christ" and what God has done for you through the blood in redemption.

18
The Atmosphere of Faith

The spirit of faith will charge the atmosphere in your house and your life. If you speak doubt and fear, it will fill the atmosphere with unbelief; but if you speak the Word, you can charge the atmosphere with faith. (The apostle Paul called it the word of faith in your mouth and your heart.)

I love to eat microwave popcorn. I like to cook it myself, because no one else can cook it just the way I do. You have to be talented to cook microwave popcorn!

I get that little bag and put it in the microwave on high. In my microwave, it takes 3 minutes and 45 seconds. While it's cooking, I get things ready in front of the television in the living room. I put a glass of water or maybe a soft drink by my chair. I make sure a good football game is on.

After one minute, I check the microwave, but nothing is happening yet. I want to sit down in the living room, but then I think, "No, I can't sit down, because I'll have to get right back up." I return to the kitchen and check the microwave. The timer is still ticking.

After two minutes, nothing is happening. After two and a half minutes, nothing is happening. I wait a little longer, and then something goes "pop." Then something else goes "pop, pop."

After 3 minutes and 20 seconds, I hear "pop, pop, pop, pop." After three minutes and 40 seconds, there's a constant popping. "Ding!" My popcorn is done. You ask, "What's the purpose of this story?"

When Nothing Is Happening

We're discussing the atmosphere of faith. When you hold fast to your confession of faith, the devil will tell you nothing is happening. Nothing may be happening *then*, but that doesn't change anything. Hold fast to your confession of faith.

One day will go by. Two days will go by. Three days will go by, and the devil will scoff, "Nothing is happening." However, on the fourth day, you'll hear a "pop" and you can say, "Glory! Something is happening. I heard a pop."

You may have believed God for 30 years, and the devil has told you that nothing is happening. Let me tell you this: In the next three months, more will happen than has happened in the last 10 or 20 years.

The devil wants you to give up on the God-kind of faith and on Christianity itself. He'll tell you, "You've been holding on to this thing for years, and it's not going to happen. You might as well give up."

You should say, "Hold on a minute! I have a measure of the God-kind of faith. I have a measure of mountain moving faith. I have overcoming faith. I speak to mountains, and they are removed. And I just heard another 'pop.' Hallelujah!"

Once my microwave popcorn went 3 minutes 45 seconds and there was no "pop." I was beginning to get really upset. I thought that maybe the microwave had a problem. But when I checked the microwave, someone had changed the setting from *high to defrost.*

If your popcorn isn't popping, you need to check the temperature. You may have been on *defrost* for the past five years. You need to crank it up to *high.*

God's Power Punch

When you launch out in faith, things happen. You are launching out, fighting the good fight of faith, and holding fast to a good confession of faith. The devil tells you it's not getting the job done, but you've got the power of the Holy Spirit. When you stretch your faith out as far as you can, the Holy Spirit shall come upon you, and God will give you a power punch.

God said that mountain will be so far gone, it will be as if it never existed. God said that tumor or cancer will disappear, and it will be as though it never was. Diabetes, high blood pressure, and arthritis will disappear and it will be as though they never afflicted you.

When you speak to old habits, emotional and mental problems, strongholds, and attitudes that have held onto you for 20 years, they will disappear. People will never know that you had that condition unless you tell them. They'll think you've always had the victory.

You'll have to tell them there once was a day when a mountain was in your way. Then you'll have to tell them what you did to get rid of it: You spoke to your mountain!

19

The Speech Center
Exercises Dominion

A leading neurosurgeon has said that the speech center in the brain exercises dominion over the whole central nervous system. He also stated that this is a recent discovery. He said you can cause different parts of the body to respond with stimuli to corresponding parts of the human brain, but when the speech center is stimulated, the whole central nervous system responds.

This means that when anyone says, "I am weak," the speech center sends out the message to the whole body to prepare to be weak. This must be the reason God said, **"Let the weak say, I am strong"** (Joel 3:10).

By Your Words
For in many things we offend all. If any man offend not in word, the same is a perfect man, and able to bridle the whole body.

James 3:2

Actually, James 3 makes it clear that the tongue controls not only the whole body, but also the desitny and quality of our lives. I like the way this passage reads in *The Message Bible*:

> **If you could find someone whose speech was perfectly true, you'd have a perfect person, in perfect control of life. A bit in the mouth of a horse controls the whole horse. A small rudder on a huge ship in the hands of a skilled captain sets course in the face of the strongest wind. A word out of your mouth may seem of no account, but it can accomplish nearly everything — or destroy it!**
>
> **James 3:2-5**

This may seem to be a new discovery in medical science, but the Bible has revealed this fact for thousands of years. Medical science is finally finding out what the Bible says has been true all along.

James 3 says the tongue will determine the *direction* and the *destination* of your life. Your tongue will also determine the *quality* of your life. First Peter 3:10 says, **"For he that will love life, and see good days, let him refrain his tongue from evil, and his lips that they speak no guile."**

You go to a doctor when something is wrong. The first thing he does is look at your tongue. When you go to God when something is wrong, the first thing God says is, "Say 'Ahh.' I see the problem. It's written all over your tongue."

The speech center is the dominion center for our lives. Our words will make us or break us. Our words determine the boundaries of our lives. Our words can limit us or loose us.

God gave Adam dominion in the beginning through the power of the spoken word, and that fact never changed. The Lord Jesus, the Last Adam, said, **"By thy words thou shalt be justified, and by thy words thou shalt be condemned"** (Matthew 12:37). Jesus also gave us the classic revelation of how faith works in Mark 11:23 where He said, **"Whosoever shall say...he shall have whatsoever he saith."** This is a fact that few people take as seriously as the Bible emphasizes.

God Touches Your Mouth To Change Your World

Anytime God wants to change anyone's life, He always touches his or her mouth. Anytime God wants to change a city or nation, He always touches someone's mouth. God changes lives through mouth-to-mouth resuscitation! He puts His words in our mouth to bring life, salvation, or healing.

God touched Isaiah's mouth with a coal of fire and sent him to speak words that would change a nation. Those words are still changing lives today — thousands of years later! God touched Jeremiah's mouth and changed his life and a nation. The list of people goes on and on, but the most important thing is that right now God is touching your mouth and changing *your* world.

Man Is a "Speaking Spirit"
And the Lord God formed man of the dust of the ground, and breathed into his nostrils the breath of life; and man became a living soul.
Genesis 2:7

A Hebrew scholar once said this verse could better be translated that man became a "speaking spirit." God created man in His own image with the capacity to speak and communicate. The power of speech was a major distinguishing factor between man and the animal kingdom.

Man was made "a speaking spirit" and given dominion. Satan also recognizes the power of spoken words and is constantly trying to get man to speak words that contaminate, defile and destroy. A constant war is going on for "air time." Satan wants to stop the spoken word of God in your personal life as well as in your city or nation.

Your Voice Is Your Ticket Out of Satan's Dominion
Say unto them, As truly as I live, saith the Lord, as you have spoken in mine ears, so will I do to you.
Numbers 14:28

The story of the nation of Israel's failure to possess the Promised Land is clearly described in Numbers 13 and 14. Everyone in these two chapters got exactly what he said. Joshua and Caleb won the war of words when they said, "We are well able to possess the land." The other leaders said "We are not able," and they died in the wilderness. Again, we can see the truth that God said, "I will do to you exactly as you said."

Words are your "address" in the spirit realm. Words are the "mail" you send out — mail that is returned to you. *Your words custom design and specifically shape your own future. Your speech center exercises dominion in your life.*

You Have Been Framed

"I have been framed." You often hear those words when working with prison inmates. Many times the person speaking doesn't realize how true those words really are. The truth is, everyone has been framed. Our words and the words of others have framed our world.

Hebrews 11:3 says that in the beginning God "framed" the worlds with His words. Everything we can see was framed with an unseen substance called *faith*. Faith is always made up of the spoken word of God. Everything we can see was made out of words and the devil has gotten into people's lives and framed a false picture that is not in God's plan.

F. F. Bosworth said, "It is impossible to boldly claim by faith a blessing that you are not sure God is offering."

You cannot boldly possess things you don't understand are available to you. If your confession is wrong, your thinking is wrong, and you do without.

As we speak the Word of God, it tears down, roots out, builds, and plants (Jeremiah 1:4–12). God wants us to speak His words and frame the picture He has for us. He has a custom plan for each of us in Christ Jesus. Ephesians 2:10 says, **"For we are his workmanship, created in Christ Jesus unto good works, which God has before ordained that we should walk in them."**

"Lego" Bible Building Blocks

Jesus said in Mark 11:23, **"Whosoever shall say...believe those things which he saith...he shall have whatsoever he saith."** He said "believe" once. He said "say, saith, saith" three times. Rev. Kenneth E. Hagin said the Lord told him he would have to do three times more teaching on the *saying* part than on the *believing* part or people wouldn't get it. The speaking part is vital to faith. Faith is released or put to work by speaking. Again, if you are silent, you lose by default.

Jesus used three different Greek words for the speaking part of faith in Mark 11:23. **"Whosover shall *say*...believe that those things which he *saith*..he shall have whatsoever he *saith*."**

The first *say* is the Greek word *epo*, which means command. It shows the authority of the believer.

The second word Jesus used is *laleo*, which means to speak out. Use your own voice. Be bold!

The third Greek word is *lego*. It means a systematic set discourse. At toy stores we see *Lego*® sets that contain bulding blocks for children to construct according to the diagram or picture on the box.

In Mark 11:22, Jesus instructs, **"Have faith in God."** He then gives us clear instructions on how faith works in Mark 11:23. He began the instructions this way, **"For verily I** *say* **unto you...."** This word *say* in Mark 11:23 is the Greek word *lego*. Jesus was constructing and giving us the building blocks to teach us how a believer's faith works.

Jesus said, "I am giving you a *lego* set of building blocks that you can use to frame your world according to the picture and diagram I have given to you in the Word of God." Actually, Jesus began by giving us a *lego*, or a way to construct our world, **"For verily I** *say* **unto you...."**

The Bible has given us a lego *set of building blocks for salvation, healing, blessing, prosperity, and victory in life. Take the Word of God and build.* Work together with God by putting His Word in your mouth and framing your future. It is not all up to your world. Your speech center exercises dominion in your life.

Your success and usefulness in this world will be measured by your confession and your tenacity to hold fast to that confession. In other words, don't just speak the confession; you must be tenacious as well.

God can be no bigger in you than you can confess Him to be. A spiritual law that few people recognize is that your words and your confessions actually shape and determine what you are and what you will become.

When I was 17 years old, I got a hold of Mark 11:23, **"Whosoever shall say unto this mountain, Be removed, and be cast into the sea, and shall not doubt in his heart but shall believe that those thing which he saith shall come to pass, he shall have whatsoever he saith."** I decided to stop *saying* what I *have* and start *having* what I *say*.

20
God's Daredevils

Every man needs a challenge. Benjamin Franklin challenged lightning and discovered electricity. The Wright brothers challenged gravity and invented the airplane. Man has challenged the heavens and walked on the Moon. He has explored the oceans, climbed the highest peaks, ridden river rapids, crossed the deserts, and scorned the Grand Canyon and Niagara Falls.

Recently I stood in the spray and deafening roar of Niagara Falls, wondering about the men who had challenged them. I had read of many daredevils who had walked tightropes strung across the foaming jaws of these powerful falls in death-defying feats.

The greatest of these daredevils was a French man named The Great Blondin, a tightrope acrobat who traveled with P. T. Barnum. When Blondin first saw Niagara Falls, excitement pulsed through his veins like a charge of electricity.

On July 4, 1859, the Frenchman walked across a 1,100 foot tightrope over the awesome current. On the same day, he crossed again, this time enclosed in a sack with only his shackled arms and legs protruding.

Every victory demanded a greater dare. Blondin performed many times before breathless spectators, each time scorning the peril. He ran across the tightrope forwards and backwards, by day and by night. He pushed a wheel barrow across, carrying a small stove, stopping midway to cook an omelette, eat part of it, and lower the rest to the astonished crowd in a boat below!

On August 3, 1859, The Great Blondin, dressed in an Indian costume, mounted the tightrope and crossed the raging, roaring river turning somersaults, suspending himself by one arm and then one leg. He stood on his head on a chair, balancing perfectly above the rushing rapids.

Another time, Blondin crossed the falls on stilts. On August 14, 1859, he asked for a volunteer to ride his back across the tightrope. His manager stepped forward. The Great Blondin strapped the man in a special harness, mounted the harness on his back, and mocked the river again. At the age of 73, Blondin successfully performed his last defiant exploit over the roaring waterfalls.

Deeds Marked by Daring and Excellence

As I stood by the falls getting soaked in the spray, my mind raced over some of the greatest challenges of time and eternity. Blondin's name was special on Earth — but was his name written in heaven?

"...The people that do know their God shall be strong, and do exploits," according to Daniel 11:32. Exploits are defined as "deeds marked by daring and excellence."

We can never know our limits or abilities unless they are tested and proven. Within our reach are unlimited possibilities with God. Jesus said in Mark 9:23, **"...all things are possible to him that believeth."**

When I was about 10 years old, we played neighborhood football games in my backyard. As the game progressed and the smaller boys were losing, the bigger boys would announce loudly, "We're going to run right up the middle." And they did!

Sometimes they ran over me. That was the height of intimidation. They said, "Here's what we're going to do. We dare you to try and stop us!" Their challenge reminds me of David, who announced to Goliath, *"I'm going to cut your head off this day"* (1 Samuel 17:46).

Rise Up and Do Exploits

Using His daredevils, God has challenged the devil throughout the Bible. God always has the stronger, bigger team. He always announces His plans beforehand.

From Jesus' birth to His death, to the resurrection, to the outpouring of the Holy Spirit, to the harvest, to the Second Coming of Jesus Christ, God prophesied all His plans ahead of time.

Then He announced, "Devil, I dare you to try to stop Me! I'm running right up the middle!"

No devil, no man, and no circumstances can stop God's divine plan for this generation. As God has declared it, we must prophesy and proclaim His power in the Earth.

He is Almighty God! He is a mighty Warrior! As we hear and know His voice, new confidence and strength come to us. We will arise with new boldness and declare His dare. It is time for a new generation of men and women to rise up and do great exploits!

21

Pioneers...Settlers...Museum Keepers

On October 14, 1947, Chuck Yeager was the first man to fly 700 miles an hour to break the sound barrier.

For many months, our military had been trying to break the 700-mile-per-hour sound barrier. It was difficult to find a man willing to risk the unknown of supersonic flight. Pilots called it the "ughknown."

Some called it the "monster" and said that no pilot or plane could withstand the stress of flying at such a speed. Others speculated that as soon as the sound barrier was broken, the airplane would disintegrate, and no pilot could survive.

Chuck Yeager volunteered. Many unsuccessful attempts were made, and many adjustments were necessary on the plane after each attempt. On the day before his successful flight, Yeager had cracked two ribs in a horseback riding accident. He had to use a sawed-off broom handle to be able to close the hatch on the X-l.

His jet was towed up to 40,000 feet by a larger plane and released. As before, his jet took off, headed for 700 mph.

No man had been there before. Yeager was determined he would be the first. As he approached 700 mph again, the plane began to rattle and shake. But Yeager was determined and pressed the throttle, pushing for 700 mph.

Suddenly, he realized he had passed the mark! Observers on the ground heard an explosion, and their hearts sank, thinking Yeager was dead. However, what they heard was a sonic boom. As they watched the sky, the X-l came back into view. Of course, they had a great celebration.

This was the beginning of America's launch into outer space and NASA's modern space shuttle. Chuck Yeager was a pioneer and became an American hero. The sound barrier everyone else was afraid of had been broken. The way into outer space was opened, and many others have followed.

A Poke Through Jell-O

Yeager said, "The real barrier wasn't in the sky, but in our knowledge and experience of supersonic flight."[1] He described the supersonic flight as "sipping lemonade on the front porch," "a poke through Jell-O," and "a perfectly paved speedway."[2]

What barriers do you face as a Christian doing the will of God? The most difficult barriers can be broken and bring us to a place in God where we have never been before.

What kind of adjustments must be made to break those barriers? Often, our own thinking, attitudes, and discipline must be changed to break the barriers.

With God's help, the greatest challenges can be "a poke through Jell-O." Then, when the barriers are broken, we can "sip lemonade on the front porch." God has not given us a spirit of fear, but of power and love and a sound mind (2 Timothy 1:7).

Breaking Barriers

There are always barriers to be broken when we go from glory to glory and from faith to faith. We will experience many breakthroughs in our lives as we overcome the enemy and fulfill all the will of God. David said that the Lord would light his candle, and by Him he could run through a troop and leap over a wall (Psalm 18:28, 29).

I have been to the First Flat-Faced Church. That is where people have tried to leap over the wall but didn't make it. They hit the wall. They have a disappointed look on their faces. They got their flat faces because they tried to leap over the wall before they got their candles lit.

David knew what it was like to face a challenge. The key is to allow God to light your candle.

The spirit of man is the candle of the Lord....
Proverbs 20:27

When your spirit is lit by God, you can break every barrier. The spirit of faith is more than just a formula; it is a fire in the spirit of man.

The revelation of the Word of God sets your spirit on fire. God's Word is the word of faith, and God is a consuming fire. The Word of God burns in your heart to enable you to overcome in every area of life. That same fire moves you from your comfort zone into greater possibilities and accomplishments.

Some people will never obey God, because they are afraid of the "ughknown." The unknown stops many from moving out into greater blessings in God. The need for security and comfort limits the ability of God to move in their lives.

Abraham, on the other hand, left his country and went out into the unknown. According to Hebrews 11:8, "By faith Abraham, when he was called to go out into a place which he should after receive for an inheritance, obeyed; and he went out, not knowing whither he went."

By faith Abraham obeyed God. Faith is obeying God even when there is an element of the unknown. Faith obeys even when you don't feel like it or know all the answers.

Proverbs 3:5, 6 says, **"Trust in the Lord with all thine heart; and lean not unto thine own understanding. In all thy ways acknowledge him, and he shall direct thy paths."**

Going Where You Have Never Been

It was necessary for Joshua to have a spirit of faith to lead the nation of Israel out of the wilderness into the Promised Land of Canaan.

And they commanded the people, saying, When ye see the ark of the covenant of the Lord your God, and the priests of the Levites bearing it, then ye shall remove from your place, and go after it. Yet there shall be a space between you and it, about two thousand cubits by measure: come not near unto it, that ye may know the way by which ye must go: for ye have not passed this way heretofore.

Joshua 3:3, 4

The people were commanded to move from their place, keep their eyes on the ark, and follow it at a certain distance. They were going into new territory. They had never passed that way before.

It seems that God led them 2,000 cubits at a time. God tells us enough to obey by faith. He doesn't tell us everything, but He tells us enough to obey. *If God told us everything, we would not have to walk by faith.*

147

God wants to take us into new territory. He wants us to go places we have never been and see things we have never seen. It takes a spirit of faith to go into the unknown.

The spirit of faith is a pioneer spirit that is not afraid of the unknown. The spirit of faith will push out from the shore and **"...Launch out into the deep...for a draught [catch]...at thy word"** (Luke 5:4, 5).

Pioneers...Settlers...Museum Keepers

There are three kinds of people: pioneers, settlers, and museum keepers.

Pioneers are continually pressing on into new territory.

Settlers stop too soon. They do not care what is beyond the next mountain. They get comfortable and never press on to the possibilities ahead. Some of the tribes of Israel settled too soon and never crossed the Jordan with Joshua.

Museum keepers are content to dust off the memories of previous generations and talk about the exploits of the past.

However, God has always had a group of pioneers who are willing to take risks and confront the devil.

22

Faith To Forsake, Follow, and Forget

A pioneer is defined as "one who ventures into unknown or unclaimed territory; one who opens up new areas; one who prepares the way."

There have been and are pioneers today in every field of human experience. We could name the pioneers in science, medicine, transportation, education, technology, and many other fields.

There also are pioneers today in the Gospel of Christ — those with the spirit of faith who are going into new territory and preparing the way for others to follow.

Between 1760 and 1850, America had a massive westward migration. Individuals and whole families loaded covered wagons pulled by oxen, horses, and mules and set out for the unknown. Stories of gold in the mountains, beautiful valleys, and unclaimed territory kept them going.

The Santa Fe Trail, the Oregon Trail, the California Trail, and many others were pioneer paths to the future. Daniel Boone, Kit Carson, Davey Crockett, and Lewis and Clark are a few of America's famous pioneers.

The pioneers had to know what to take and what to leave behind. Only the most necessary items were allowed. Often the trails were cluttered with things people had to leave behind to make it across the deserts or over the mountains. It was a long journey, and the main rule of every wagon trail was "keep moving."

Many people — especially small children, women, the elderly, and the infirm — died along the way, but the pioneers had to keep moving. They always had an expectation about what lay ahead.

Pioneers in the Gospel

God is always looking for pioneers — people who will not settle for less than God's best. The spirit of faith will keep them moving, and the pioneers will keep expecting miracles. The spirit of faith is not afraid to leave things behind.

There are some things that weigh us down and hinder us from making it over the next mountain to the next level of faith and glory. It can be difficult to lay aside treasured items and traditional ways of thinking, but the rewards of obeying God keep us moving.

"By faith, Moses forsook Egypt," Hebrews 11:27 says. It takes faith to forsake the ways of this world and walk in the ways of God. It takes faith to walk away from the pleasures and temptations of this world. Moses did it by faith.

When he was 75 years old, Abraham forsook Ur of the Chaldees to go to Canaan (Genesis 11:31-12:9). Abraham kept moving. Peter, James, and John forsook their boats and followed Jesus (Mark 1:17,1 8). It takes faith to forsake and faith to follow.

It also takes faith to forget the past (Hebrews 11:15). If you keep looking back, you can't go forward. That is why God said, **"Remember ye not the former things...I will do a new thing; now it shall spring forth...I will even make a way in the wilderness, and rivers in the desert"** (Isaiah 43:18, 19).

The apostle Paul said, **"...forgetting those things which are behind, and reaching forth unto those things which are before, I press toward the mark...."** (Philippians 3:13, 14).

The Glory Road

I heard someone prophesy by the Holy Spirit about two roads that lie ahead. The prophecy was:

"One road goes out ahead and is straight and clear, and you can see what lies ahead, and it looks really nice. That is 'The Blessing Road.' You can take that road and see the blessing of God in a measure in your life.

"However, there is another road that goes a different direction up a high mountain. It winds around, and you cannot see what is around the next bend. The mountain looks rugged and rough. When you look at that road, you say, 'I sure don't want that road,' but that is the road you should take.

"That is 'The Glory Road.' There is much sacrifice, and it is much more challenging, but when you get to the top and see what is on the other side, you will be glad you chose that road. The glory of God is to be seen by those who choose this road."

It takes a spirit of faith to choose The Glory Road. Many just want the blessing and want the road that requires the least effort. God is good, and He will bless us as much as He can. There is, however, a choice to make when we want to see the glory of God. The spirit of faith always chooses The Glory Road.

Mountain Moving and Mountain Climbing

The spirit of faith moves the mountains that are hindrances to our receiving from God. The spirit of faith also climbs the mountain that represents our obedience to the will of God.

Who shall ascend into the hill of the Lord? or who shall stand in his holy place? He that hath clean hands, and a pure heart; who hath

not lifted up his soul unto vanity, nor sworn deceitfully. He shall receive the blessing from the Lord....

Psalm 24:3-5

The *Knox* translation says, **"Who dares climb the mountain of the Lord?"**

The Glory Road is like climbing the mountain of the Lord. It is like a spiritual Mount Everest. It requires clean hands and a pure heart. It requires training and discipline to make it to the top. However, the rewards at the top make the journey worthwhile. The glory of God can be seen and experienced by those who choose The Glory Road.

A few of the people who have taken The Glory Road are: David Livingston, Hudson Taylor, Lillian Trasher, P. C. Nelson, William Seymour, Smith Wigglesworth, Lilian B. Yeomans, Martin Luther, John Wesley, Lester Sumrall, Aimee Semple McPherson, and many others.

In every generation, many choose The Glory Road to find the divine destiny God has for them. The spirit of faith blazes a pioneer path for others to follow their faith and receive God's best blessings.

There are three kinds of people:

PIONEERS, SETTLERS, and MUSEUM KEEPERS.

Museum keepers are content to dust off the memories of the past.

Settlers are content to stay in their comfort zone.

Pioneers are constantly pressing into new territories.

23

The Pioneer Advance of the Gospel

The apostle Paul wrote the letter to the Philippians from prison in Rome. He mentions *joy* or *rejoicing* 16 times in four short chapters.

Paul was a happy man, even in the worst circumstances. He had a spirit of faith. He thanked the believers at Philippi for their partnership in the Gospel. He was not only thanking them; he also was blessing them with a word from God that guaranteed every one of their needs met because of their giving (Philippians 4:19).

There is another aspect in this letter that concerns the furtherance of the Gospel. In Philippians 1:12, Paul wrote, **"But I would ye should understand, brethren, that the things which happened unto me have fallen out rather unto the furtherance of the gospel."**

The word "furtherance" could be translated "the pioneer advance of the Gospel." It means "to go into new territory." Paul was rejoicing about the advance of the Gospel. The Philippian believers were partners with Paul in the pioneer advance of the Gospel. Even though they remained in Philippi, their pioneer spirit of faith was expressed through their giving.

The Gospel of Christ is not meant for a museum; it is for us today. It is full of power and expansion. "Settlers" put too many limits on the Gospel, because the Gospel is unlimited. We may not see all the results of the spirit of faith during our lifetime. It keeps going, growing, and advancing.

Jesus is the original Pioneer. He is the Author and the Finisher of our faith (Hebrews 12:1, 2). He left heaven and pioneered the union of God and man. His sacrifice on the cross and His resurrection joined us to Him through faith.

Paul uses the word "furtherance" again in Philippians 1:25: **"And having this confidence, I know that I shall abide and continue with you all for your furtherance and joy of faith."**

Believers should continue to advance in the joy of faith. We should go into new areas of joy and believing. The spirit of faith is ever-increasing faith and ever-increasing joy.

History's Hidden Turning Point

The spirit of faith is evident in the apostle Paul's life and ministry. Paul's three missionary journeys were exploits in Christ that changed the world.

An article from the April 22, 1991 issue of *U.S. News and World Report*, by Gerald Parshall, caught my attention.

In the middle years of the first century, preachers of many religions and philosophical stripes traveled the sea lanes and cobblestone roads of the eastern Roman Empire. Among them was an indefatigable evangelist in a rough coat and crude sandals who supported himself in his missionary work by making tents. Contemporary historians did not deem him worthy of a single mention, having no inkling of how great a tent maker Paul of Tarsus was. They could not know that he was erecting the theological tent of Christianity, making it broad enough to accommodate all manner of humankind, to girdle the globe and to survive two millenniums as a major force in history.

While Paul traveled by foot, by donkey, by horseback and by boat across Asia Minor and Macedonia establishing new congregations, he reinforced his gospel to previous converts with a series of letters that have awed even secular historians. Will Durant called them "among the most forceful and eloquent...in all literature."[1]

This article was a part of a larger article entitled "History's Hidden Turning Points" by Daniel J. Boorstin, who wrote, "The true watersheds in human affairs are seldom spotted quickly amid the tumult of headlines broadcast on the hour."[2]

The apostle Paul played a tremendous role in a major turning point in history. The spirit of faith enabled him to obey the "heavenly vision" and change the world. Paul called it "the same spirit of faith."

Today, those who follow Jesus catch the same spirit of faith. We also believe, speak, and establish hidden turning points in people around the world.

24

See You at the Top

I recently viewed a documentary videotape about Mount Everest and those who have climbed it. As you may know, Mount Everest is the tallest mountain in the world.

I was inspired by the challenges of climbing to the top of the world. The first men to successfully make it to the top were Sir Edmund Hillary and Tenzing Norgay in 1953.

Since then, more than 700 people from around the world have made it to the top of Mount Everest. Many have tried and failed, and yet others have lost their lives on the treacherous mountain.

One of the most interesting facts is that climbers cannot go immediately from the bottom to the top, because it is physically impossible for the body to adjust to the thin air or the lack of oxygen in a short period of time. If someone were to try it, he would die.

The process of climbing the mountain takes the mountain-climbers from lower camps to higher camps as they gradually make the ascent. Sometimes they stay at high altitude camps for as long as three weeks until their bodies adjust to the high altitude.

During this process, their red blood cells actually double in number to be able to carry enough oxygen to keep them alive. This kind of mountain-climbing must be in your blood in order for you to survive!

As I watched the video about Mount Everest, I thought of Psalm 24:3, 4: **"Who shall ascend into the hill of the Lord? or who shall stand in his holy place? He that hath clean hands, and a pure heart...."** The *Knox* translation says, **"Who dares climb the mountain of the Lord...."**[1]

In these verses, God is giving a challenge to anyone who wants to move up higher in their fellowship with Him. After He gives the condition of clean hands and a pure heart, He gives the promise of "receiving the blessing from the Lord."

There are some blessings you cannot receive from God at sea level. You must move up higher in God's presence. As you do, you make adjustments to the altitude. You also make adjustments in your *attitude*.

The precious blood of Jesus is applied for cleansing, and double red blood cells carry much-needed oxygen for you to finish your course. The blood of Jesus provides "the double cure" for soul and body.

"This is the generation of them that seek him, that seek thy face, O God of Jacob," David wrote in Psalm 24:6. This ascension into God's holy place brings you face-to-face with Jesus. You stand in His presence and are forever changed. You find your place face-to-face with Him.

This is a much greater challenge than climbing Mount Everest. The Mountain of the Lord is a much higher calling than the challenges or the achievements of this world.

This is the true hunger in the heart of every believer, and this is where satisfaction, fulfillment, and blessings flow.

It is time for us to move up higher in the glory of God. The Holy Spirit is our Guide, and He will take us to the top if we will listen to Him and follow Him.

See you at the top!

Faith works by love.

A step
out of love
is a step
out of God.

KENNETH E. HAGIN

25
Unforgiveness:
The Biggest Enemy to Faith

No book on faith would be complete without dealing with the greatest hindrance to faith: unforgiveness.

> **Jesus answering saith unto them, Have faith in God.**
>
> **Mark 11:22**

A marginal note reads, "Have the faith of God. Have the God-kind of faith."

> **For verily I say unto you, That whosoever shall say unto this mountain, Be thou removed, and be thou cast into the sea; and shall not doubt in his heart, but shall believe that those things which he saith shall come to pass; he shall have whatsoever he saith.**
>
> **Mark 11:23**

> **Therefore I say unto you, What things soever ye desire, when ye pray, believe that ye receive them, and ye shall have them.**
>
> **Mark 11:24**

Jesus was talking about faith in verse 22, how to release your faith in your saying in verse 23, and how to release your faith in your praying in verse 24. In the following two verses, He said that the biggest enemy to faith in your life is unforgiveness or offense.

> **And when ye stand praying, forgive, if ye have ought against any: that your Father also which is in heaven may forgive you your trespasses. But if ye do not forgive, neither will your Father which is in heaven forgive your trespasses.**
>
> **Mark 11:25, 26**

Notice Jesus said, "...if ye have *ought* against any." "Ought" is holding a grudge against someone about anything. A grudge implies some sort of bitterness. The Bible speaks of "a root of bitterness" that defiles people (Hebrews 12:15).

When the Devil Works on You

The biggest enemy to faith is unforgiveness. In Mark 11, Jesus was talking about moving mountains. He said all things are possible in prayer. However, He pointed out that if you don't deal with unforgiveness, none of your praying, your saying, or your faith will work!

The devil knows that he can neutralize your faith with unforgiveness faster than any other way. Unforgiveness is the door through which he enters.

Brother Kenneth E. Hagin said it this way: "Anytime you're feeling mistreated, you know that the devil is working on you." Watch it, because those feelings and that voice will come to you and say, "You've been mistreated" if someone did you wrong or said something you didn't like. The devil will continue to work on you to set up an offense.

If someone really did you wrong, you must forgive him by releasing him of any unforgiveness on your part. You must not speak against him or attack him, and you must let go of your unforgiveness. When you release him, forgive him. And when you forgive him, something positive will happen inside you.

I like what Smith Wigglesworth said: "I realize that God can never bless us on the lines of being hardhearted, critical, or unforgiving. This will hinder faith quicker than anything will. I believe there are a great many people who would be healed, but they are harboring things in their hearts that are as a blight. Let these things go. Forgive and the Lord will forgive you. There are many good people, people that mean well, but they have no power to do anything for God. There is just some little thing that came in their hearts years ago and their faith has been paralyzed since."

Faith Works by Love

Galatians 5:6 says, **"...faith which worketh by love."** Your faith life will not work properly if you are not walking in love. Faith worketh by love!

165

So if your mountain keeps standing there in the same old place, and you're not receiving what you're praying for — if your faith is not working — the first thing you need to check is your love walk.

The problem is not with God. Check your love walk. Evaluate the way you're talking and acting and the way you are conducting your relationships. Walk in love, because faith works by love.

How long does it take to deal with an offense or unforgiveness? If it's something that both you and the other person know about, you will have to deal with him or her.

You may argue, "What if I tell him I'm sorry, but I feel like it's really his fault, and he won't tell me he's sorry?" Even if that person doesn't reciprocate, it's not your business. It's not your business to make him forgive. Your business is to forgive him!

Get rid of that grudge! When another person is involved and knows about the problem, you need to say, "I want you to forgive me."

Forgiveness Is Your Responsibility

However, if the other person doesn't know about the problem — if it's something you did or something you've been holding against him — there's no reason to get him involved, because you'll stir up more devils than you can cast out!

Don't tell that person, "I've been mad at you for six months" when he doesn't know it. Just forgive him and be friendly again.

Ephesians 4:26 says you shouldn't let the sun go down on your wrath. What does that mean? One translation says, "Don't let the sun go down finding you nursing a grudge." This is where the devil has his greatest opportunity to hinder your faith from working.

Ephesians 4:27 continues, "Neither give place to the devil." If the devil has any place in your life, you gave it to him! Of course, you might have given it to him ignorantly. You might not have known what you were doing, or you might have given him place through negligence. In other words, you refused to do what is right. Negligence means you refused to exercise your authority as a believer.

Another way the devil got in was through disobedience. You knew what the Word says, and you refused to do it. Thus, you opened the door to the devil.

Old Testament Examples

As you study Job in the Old Testament, you will notice that God turned his captivity when he prayed for his friends (Job 42:10). Job's friends were really his critics. God can turn your captivity, too, if you will pray for your critics and ask God to bless them.

Joseph is the greatest illustration of God's promotion. He had many opportunities for offense during his life. His brothers cast him into a pit and sold him into slavery; in Egypt, Potiphar's wife falsely accused him of rape; and the two men he helped get released from prison refused to speak up for him (Genesis 37, 39, and 40).

Joseph could have turned into a bitter, mean, and frustrated man, but the Bible says that while he was in prison, Joseph willingly did whatever the jailer needed with all his might. So even while he was in prison, Joseph kept on working as unto the Lord, and he never got bitter.

God brought him out of prison, turned the whole situation around, and made him ruler over all of Egypt. Eventually his brothers came to Egypt and knelt down before him, begging to buy food in the middle of a severe drought. He could have said, "I've got a chance to get you back now for what you did to me 20 years ago," but he never held that grudge. Instead, he told his brothers, "What you meant for evil God turned for my good. Now I can be a blessing to you."

Joseph was promoted by God, but if he had let unforgiveness and bitterness enter his heart, God could never have taken him where He needed him to go as ruler of Egypt.

Offenses will come. You need to guard against them. One minister said, "Life is not fair, but God is good."

Unforgiveness Can Cause Disease

Injustices and other problems that happen in life might not have been your responsibility. Something someone else did may cause you to be in a pit. Keep remembering that God is good, and He will bring you out. Guard against bitterness. Remember, unforgiveness is the greatest enemy to your faith, so you must deal with it quickly.

I believe that we will never find a cure for certain diseases, because all diseases are not simply physical or biological. Some have their roots in a curse or breaking a spiritual law. That means the devil is the source of it all!

When he tricks you into being unforgiving or bitter, all kinds of incurable diseases may result. Medicine won't be able to cure these diseases, because the cure for them is spiritual. Sometimes you will have to deal with something in your heart before you can receive your healing. *The cure for certain diseases is forgiveness!*

Guard Your Heart

Often people let things eat on them for years and years. But Jesus said, "When you stand praying, forgive." This means, while you are standing praying, you can quickly make an adjustment in your heart.

You can make a decision to forgive. Forgiveness is not a feeling; it's a choice. You may still have feelings of hurt, but you make a decision to forgive. You can forgive.

God forgives you of your sins and trespasses. On the cross, Jesus said, "Father, forgive them." He was telling God to forgive people who had been beating him, spitting on Him, and mocking him.

Faith is of the heart. That's the reason why unforgiveness is a disease of the heart. That spirit will get inside you and make your heart callused so your faith won't respond or work properly. Then you will get cynical, and you won't be able to receive from God.

First, the devil is trying to keep your faith from working. Second, he is trying to get you to open the door to unforgiveness. If the devil can get in through unforgiveness, sickness will follow — and remain. Poverty will enter, and you won't be able to get rid of it. Then the door is open for other problems. That's why you need to close the door of unforgiveness and offense.

Unforgiveness — offense and bitterness — is the primary thing you have to guard against. You must watch out for unforgiveness just as if it were a rattlesnake. When you see it come around, avoid it!

Furthermore, don't pick up the offense of someone else. If the devil can't get you offended, he'll make someone close to you get offended so you will pick up his or her offense.

The Peace of God

Psalm 119:165 says, "Great peace have they which love thy law: and nothing shall offend them." The word "offense" means a place of stumbling — something that trips you up. When you love the Lord, the peace of God is yours, and you decide nothing is going to trip you up.

The old saying is that to err is human, and to forgive is divine. What that means is this: We don't live in a perfect world, and we never will. People make mistakes, and they always will — and so will you. So you may as well go ahead and forgive others.

Jesus said the amount of forgiveness you dish out is the amount you will get in return (Matthew 7:2). Therefore, you ought to dish out as much forgiveness as you can, because you'll probably need it.

Be careful when you are judging others or you see someone fall in a certain area of life. Don't say, "I would never do that." In six months, you'll do something worse than that! Jesus said in Matthew 7:1, **"Judge not, that ye be not judged."** Then He said, **"Stop criticizing others."**

Read First Corinthians 13, the great Love Chapter. Draw the love line out and walk on it. Faith works by love, but the primary enemy of faith is unforgiveness. Remember, forgiveness is not a feeling; it's a choice!

Endnotes

Chapter 1

[1]E. W. Kenyon, *The Two Kinds of Life* (Kenyon's Publishing Society, 1997), p. 59.

[2]Ruth Ward Heflin, *Glory* (Hagerstown, MD, The McDougal Publishing Company, 1990), p. 136.

[3]Michael D. Lemonick, "What's Hiding in the Quarks," *Time* magazine, Vol. 147, No. 8, February 19, 1996, p. 54.

[4]Lilian B. Yeomans, M.D., *The Great Physician* (Springfield, MO: Gospel Publishing House, 1933), p. 64.

[5]The Lockman Foundation, *The Amplified Bible* (Grand Rapids, MI: Zondervan Bible Publishers, 1958), p. 352.

[6]Clarence Jordan, *The Cotton Patch Version of Hebrews and the General Epistles* (New York, NY: Association Press, 1973), p. 35.

Chapter 2

[1]Matt Cartmill, "The Gift of Gab," *Discover* magazine, Vol. 19, No. 11, November 1998), p. 56.

Chapter 3

[1]Mark Hankins, *The Power of Identification With Christ* (Alexandria, LA: Mark Hankins Publications, 1998), pp. v-vi.

Chapter 4

[1]Lilian B. Yeomans, M.D., *The Great Physician* (Springfield, MO: Gospel Publishing House, 1933), p. 64.

Chapter 5

[1]Don Gossett and E. W. Kenyon, *The Power of Your Words* (Blaine, WA: Don and Joyce Gossett, 1977), p. 32

[2]The Lockman Foundation, *The Amplified Bible* (Grand Rapids, MI: Zondervan Bible Publishers, 1958), p. 364.

Chapter 7

[1]Lilian B. Yeomans, M.D., *The Great Physician* (Springfield, MO: Gospel Publishing House, 1933), p. 31.

Chapter 9
[1]*Ibid*: p. 31.

Chapter 10
[1]Lilian B. Yeomans, M.D., *Balm of Gilead* (Springfield, MO: Gospel Publishing House, 1936), pp. 21-23.

Chapter 11
[1]Lilian B. Yeomans, M.D., *The Great Physician* (Springfield, MO: Gospel Publishing House, 1933), p. 19.

Chapter 13
[1]The Lockman Foundation, *The Amplified Bible* (Grand Rapids, MI: Zondervan Bible Publishers, 1958), p. 86.

Chapter 15
[1]Lilian B. Yeomans, M.D., *The Great Physician* (Springfield, MO: Gospel Publishing House, 1933), p. 22.

Chapter 21
[1]Gen. Chuck Yeager and Leo Janos, *Yeager* (New York, NY: Bantam Books, 1985), p. 130.
[2]*Ibid*: p. 130

Chapter 22
[1]Msgr. Ronald A. Knox, *The Shorter Knox Bible* (London, England: Macmillan and Company Unlimited, 1958), p. 248.

Chapter 23
[1]Gerald Parshall, "The Momentous Mission of the Apostle Paul," *U.S. News & World Report*, Vol. 110, No. 15, April 22, 1991, pp. 54-55.
[2]Daniel J. Boorstin, "History's Hidden Turning Points," *U.S. News & World Report*, Vol. 110, No. 15, April 22, 1991, p. 52.

Chapter 24
[1]Msgr. Ronald A. Knox, *The Shorter Knox Bible* (London, England: Macmillan and Company Unlimited, 1958), p. 248.

RESOURCES

To purchase items
or for more information
please contact:

MARK HANKINS MINISTRIES
P.O. BOX 12863
ALEXANDRIA, LA 71315

PHONE: **318.448.4500**
FAX: **318.767.2001**

e-mail: **hankinsmin@aol.com**

visit us on the web
www.markhankins.org

AUTHOR

Mark Hankins is the pastor of Christian Worship Center in Alexandria, Louisiana. He travels extensively throughout the United States and overseas preaching the Gospel with the power of God for people today in revivals, seminars, and campmeetings.

Pastor Hankins has a daily television program "The Spirit of Faith," and his radio program, "Taking Your Place In Christ" is heard in many parts of the United States as well as around the world via the internet. His message centers on redemption in Christ and who the believer is in Christ.

Other books by Pastor Hankins:

Taking Your Place In Christ

Spirit-Filled Scripture Study Guide

The Power of Identification With Christ

11:23 The Language of Faith

The Spirit of Faith

Acknowledging Every Good Thing That Is in You In Christ

Never Run at your Giant with your Mouth Shut